Researching Your U.S. WWI Army Ancestors

Margaret M. McMahon, Ph.D.

Copyright © 2016 by Dr. Margaret M. McMahon. All rights reserved. No part of this may be reproduced in any manner whatsoever without written permission, except in the case of brief quotations in articles and reviews. All trademarks or copyrights mentioned herein are the possession of their respective owners and the author makes no claim of ownership by mention of products that contain these marks.

Disclaimer
The author has no commercial connection with any of the trademark holders.

ISBN: **1537648926**
ISBN-13: **978-1537648927**

DEDICATION

This book is dedicated to both my Grandfathers who served in World War I, Joseph F. McMahon and Arthur H. Gilroy. As the centennial of their involvement in the Great War approaches, my thoughts have turned to them and the dark days their world faced.

Books by

Margaret M. McMahon

A Week of Genealogy

A Weekend of Genealogy

CONTENTS

	Acknowledgments	vii
1	Introduction	1
2	Background	3
3	Timelines	7
4	Get Started	11
5	Individual Military Records	13
6	Finding Records Online	17
7	Cemeteries	22
8	Battles	26
9	Books	29
10	American Memory Collection	33
11	Maps	37
12	Photos and Videos	40
13	Archives	48
14	Newspapers	60
15	Ephemera	65
16	Museums	72
17	Social Networking	84
18	Putting It All Together	89

19	To France and Back	93
20	Google	98
21	Concluding Thoughts	100

ACKNOWLEDGMENTS

Special thanks goes to the research specialists at the U.S. Army Heritage and Education Center for their help, guidance and enthusiasm. Thanks also to the specialists and staff at the National Archives and Records Administration II in College Park, MD.

I appreciate all those who have attended my lectures and read my books for their encouragement during this project.

Thanks to Sharon Gumerove and the Sonic Digital Design, LLC, for outstanding technical services.

As always, thanks to my dependable research assistants and enthusiasts, the Michaels.

1 INTRODUCTION

My Grandfather, Joseph F. McMahon, was born on 29 August 1894 in Kilrush, County Clare, Ireland. He arrived in the U.S. on 6 October 1907 with his widowed Mother and the youngest siblings. Sadly, he died when my Father was a young child, and was never able to share his stories. Through this research into his military service, my goal was to learn about him and the stories that he might have told. By using the resources and methodology described in this book, I learned more about what a year of his life was like. The records of the 51st Pioneer Infantry and the American Expeditionary Forces that are held in multiple Archives, and in other collections, were used follow him from his induction into the Army, to France and in battle, then to the occupation of Germany, and finally back to his discharge from the Army in the U.S. It was as if I had collected the materials for a scrapbook of memories similar to what his would have been.

    As I researched his life, I learned that many of my preconceived notions were incorrect. The most notable misconceptions were corrected: my Grandfather became a citizen before his military service in WWI, and he married my Grandmother prior to leaving for war. I did not know how they met, but the 1920 U.S. Census provided me a clue because both were recorded as being employed as clerks in the Western Union Telegraph office.

    Through researching his military service, I learned that my Grandfather and my Father shared common experiences in their different wars. My Father had never known that both he and his

Father had German soldiers surrender to them in a World War. For my Grandfather it was in France; for my Father it was in Greenland.

This book was written as my research progressed. My popular lectures about military research and using military archives became the core of this work. This book contains material that is suitable not only for beginners but also for more advanced researchers. It begins with the research that can be done by beginners, but as the chapters progress, the concepts become more suitable for intermediate researchers. However, do not let that dissuade you; by pursuing these techniques you may push your skills to the next level.

While this book is specifically about U.S. Army ancestors, the same techniques can be used to research ancestors who served in the U.S. Marine Corps and the U.S. Navy during World War I.

Through military records, history, maps, documents and artifacts you can learn more about your ancestor's WWI experience. This book can guide you to locating those sources, and suggest ways to combine and share what you find.

2 BACKGROUND

We know it as World War I, but back then it was the first and only global conflict. It was the Great War. It was supposed to be the War to End All Wars.

Army Infantrymen and Marines who served in the Great War were known as Doughboys. There is no agreement about how the term came to be used, but there are many theories. One theory is from the Mexican-American War of 1846-48 and is based on the fact soldiers' uniforms were often covered with dust. That dust looked like the adobe used to form the unbaked bricks that are used as the building blocks of structures in the Southwest. Another theory is the large buttons on the uniforms were said to look like dough cakes. Yet another theory relates to the flour and rice mixtures that formed dough. Soldiers wrapped the dough around a stick or a bayonet and cooked it in a flame.

Your ancestor may have begun his military service as part of his state's National Guard. These troops were federalized during the war, and state guard regiments may have been reorganized into army regiments and renamed. For example, the New York Tenth Infantry was reformed as the 51st Pioneer Infantry. A soldier may have stayed with others from his state, or may have been transferred to other groups.

When researching doughboy ancestors, your grade school knowledge of World War I may help to put the soldier's service into context. Here are some dates of interest:
- 28 Jun 1914 Archduke Ferdinand is assassinated.

- 28 July 1914 the war begins.
- 16 Jan 1917 the Zimmerman Telegraph is sent from the German Foreign Office proposing a military alliance with Mexico. The message was coded and the U.S. Embassy in Berlin agreed to transmit it because the German telegraph cables had been cut.
- 6 Apr 1917 The U.S. declares war on Germany.
- 26 May 1917 The first U.S. troops arrive in France.
- 5 Jun 1917 The U.S. has National Draft Registration Day.
- 11 Nov 1918 There is an armistice between the Allies and Germany.
- 28 Jun 1919 The Treaty of Versailles is signed.
- 3 Jan 1920 The last U.S. Troops in France leave.
- 24 Jan 1923 The last U.S. occupation troops leave Germany.

The U.S. entered the war years after it had begun. For those whose Army ancestors who served overseas, they became part of the American Expeditionary Forces (AEF) from the time they left American soil.

You may find that your ancestor's unit was attached to a French or English army. Troops from the U.S. were often attached to existing military groups. It was not until the Battle of Saint-Mihiel that the U.S. led its own troops into battle. The 33rd Infantry Division, also known as the Prairie Division, had the distinction of being the only military formation that was attached to French, English and American forces.

The war ended quickly after the U.S. troops arrived in Europe. The Armistice between Germany and the Allies went into effect on the eleventh hour (Paris time), of the eleventh day, of the eleventh month in 1918. After that, there were troops that still served in the occupation of Germany.

The largest unit of organization of the AEF was an Army. There were multiple Armies; each consisting of two or more Corps. Each Corps was made up of two or more Divisions. In the AEF, a Division would have three Regiments (Figure 1). Each Regiment contained infantrymen, organized into companies. The Regiment also contained machine gun, artillery, engineering, logistical and other support units. Companies might be further divided into platoons. There were Headquarter Companies, Supply Companies, and Companies identified by letters. Keep these organizations in mind as you study history to understand what your ancestor might have been doing, and where.

Military histories may contain specifics of how military groups are organized, which is the Order of Battle. Wikipedia has an article about the AEF Order of Battle for the Western Front at: https://en.wikipedia.org/wiki/American_Expeditionary_Forces_on_the_Western_Front_(World_War_I)_order_of_battle. An example of this military structure was the First Army, organized and led by General John J. Pershing. At the time of the St. Mihiel Offensive it contained I Corps, IV Corps, V Corps, and the French II Colonial Corps. I Corps contained the 1st, 2nd, 26th, 32nd, 41st and 42nd Infantry Divisions. Each of these Divisions was made up of multiple Brigades. The 2nd Infantry Division contained the 3rd Infantry, 2nd Field Artillery and 4th Marine Brigades. The 4th Marine Brigade contained the 5th and 6th Regiments and the 6th Machine Gun Battalion. Brigades included Infantry Regiments, Field Artillery Regiments, Trench Mortar Batteries, and/or Machine Gun Battalions.

There were multiple Armies organized in WWI. During the Occupation of Germany after the war, for example, the Third Army was composed of the III Corps and the IV Corps.

While some soldiers were always assigned to the same Division and Army, some groups were moved around to support the different Armies. For example, my Grandfather was in the 51st Pioneer Infantry Regiment (PIR), Company B. At different times the 51st PIR was attached to the 4th, 6th, and 3rd Armies.

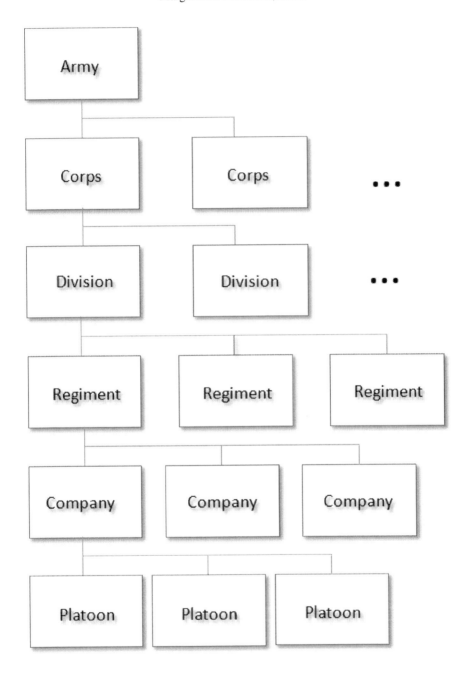

Figure 1. Organization of the AEF.

3 TIMELINES

A timeline is a useful tool for keeping your research on track. Your ancestor's timeline may begin with something as simple as the dates of the U.S. involvement in WWI, which are shown in the Introduction. You can start the timeline even if all you know are the soldier's dates of service.

When you find a service summary for your ancestor (Figure 2), use the data you extract from it to fill in the timeline.

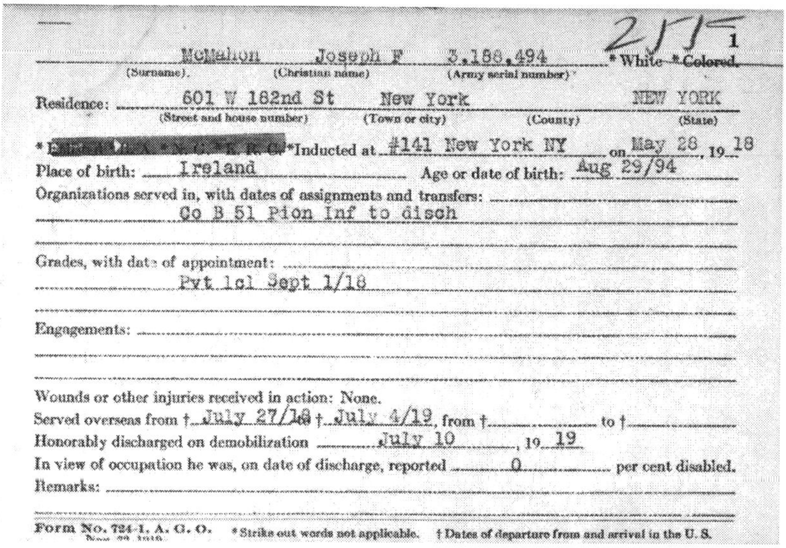

Figure 2. New York State Service Summary Card for Joseph McMahon.

From the summary shown in Figure 2, I could begin to construct a timeline of Joseph McMahon's military life during World War I.

Joseph F. McMahon Timeline Service (Co. B 51st PIR)

28 May 1918	Inducted @141 New York, NY
27 July 1918	Leaves for overseas
1 Sep 1918	Pvt 1cl
4 July 1919	Return from overseas
10 July 1919	Discharge (Final Payment Roll)

Combining the information that I found in several Google searches, I then compiled more timeline data. Some of the data you find may overlap or be contradictory, because different companies of a Regiment might be involved in different activities. Within companies, platoons or groups might have different assignments. At this point I did not know the movements or actions specifically involving Company B of the 51st Pioneer Infantry of New York. I combined these items into a cheat sheet that proved useful during online searches and in-person visits to archives (Figure 3).

Joseph F. McMahon – Timeline of Service　　**Co B 51 Pioneer Infantry**
28 May 1918　　　　　　　　　　　　　　　Inducted @141 New York, NY
27 July 1918　　　　　　　　　　　　　　　Leaves for overseas
1 Sep 1918　　　　　　　　　　　　　　　　Pvt 1cl
4 July 1919　　　　　　　　　　　　　　　　Return from overseas
10 July 1919　　　　　　　　　　　　　　　 Discharge (Final Payment Roll)

- The 51st was a New York National Guard Regiment, reorganized as a Pioneer Infantry.
- The 51st Pioneer Infantry was formerly the 10th New York Infantry (National Guard).
- 4 JAN 1918 The 10th NY Infantry was re-designated 51st Pioneer Regiment; 1st NY Infantry was re-designated 1st Pioneer Regiment
- The 51st Pioneer Infantry was composed of 39 officers and 904 enlisted men after reorganization. It was commanded by Colonel J. Guy Deming and filled to wartime strength with draftees.
- They were organized in Jan 1918 in Camp Wadsworth, SC as corps troops unit
- These troops were not part of any Division; they were attached when needed to an American Army or Corps.
- The regiment left Camp Wadsworth on 17 July 1918 with 3545 officers and men.
- They went overseas in Jul 1918
- 29 JUL 1918 Left Camp Wadsworth for Port of New Jersey Steamer "KROONLAND" to France
- They served with IV Army Corps Aug-Sep 1918
- 8 AUG 1918 arrive Brest, France
- Assigned to Corps Engineers, 4th Army Corps, US AEF
- The 51st (and 1st) Pioneer Infantry Regiments served as Corps Engineer support with the 4th Corps.
- They served with First Army Sep 1918
- They served with IV and VI Army Corps Sep-Nov 1918
- 12 SEP 1918 St. Mihiel campaign
- They were with the Third Army on the Rhine occupation
- They returned to the U.S. in Jul 1919
- They were demobilized at Camp Upton, New York

Figure 3. Example Cheat Sheet.

A Station List enumerates where a military organization was on each day. These were found at NARA II and will be discussed in Chapter 13. When I added the data from the Station List for Company B, 51st Pioneer Infantry Regiment (Figure 4) to the timeline for Joseph McMahon, the details expanded what I knew about his story.

Take the time to transcribe key information in the Station List, so that it can be included in the timeline or used in your narrative.

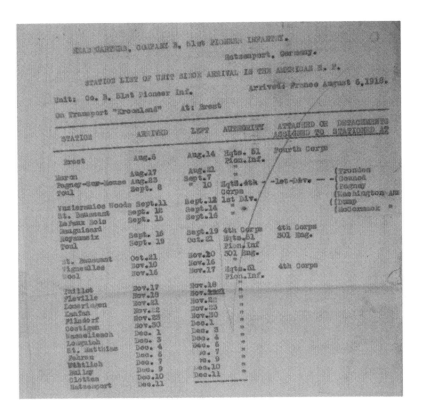

Figure 4. Station List for Company B, 51st Pioneer Infantry Regiment (NARA, RG 165 Box 51st Pioneer Infantry Regiment, Box 439, Folder 1).

4 GET STARTED

Start by determining your ancestor's branch of service. The first place to look for this information is in your home. You may have the ancestor's individual military records, images, or other memorabilia. Continue the scope of your search by asking immediate family members and other relatives to look through their homes. You might find a cousin has inherited a photo of your ancestor in uniform.

After identifying the branch of service, look for material about his military organization, especially the Regiment in which your ancestor served. Similarly, look for information about the ships upon which your naval ancestors served.

Then it is time to learn about the history of the Great War. Find the history of the groups with which he served, and from there learn about the battles in which he was involved.

Capture the information in a timeline, using what you know, and fill in that timeline with dates and events as you gather new information about the individual's service, the military unit's activities, and events through the eyes of their comrades.

Print out the timeline with its useful information to keep as a cheat sheet as you go through records. An example was shown in Figure 3. This will help you stay on track as you investigate the records during your ancestor's time with a military unit, or in a geographic location. This sheet was a very helpful reference when I visited archives and museums.

During our ancestors' time, the war was known as the Great War and the War to End All Wars, and not World War I. Keep that in mind when you are searching the contemporary sources.

5 INDIVIDUAL MILITARY RECORDS

When you search for information about an individual's military service, consider the events in a person's military career. The military events in a service member's life span from draft registration to burial.

Military records are generated for draft registration, induction, military service, discharge, post-service, and death.

Draft registration cards provide genealogical information. Men could have registered for the draft and not entered the military. Therefore, you should always look for draft registration cards whether or not your ancestor served in the military. Look for the World War I draft registration cards at Ancestry.com or Rootsweb (Figure 5). The draft board officials tore off the lower left corner for African-American registrants to indicate they were to be assigned to segregated units.

After an ancestor was drafted, he received an induction notice. This may be one of the papers you find in yours or a relative's home.

During the period of an ancestor's military service, he may have been promoted, or received medals or honors. There may be information about the these events at home, in service summaries or in newspapers. During WWI, the Army kept individual official military personnel files (OMPF), but many of them were burned in 1973 by a fire at the National Personnel Records Center (NPRC) of the National Archives in St. Louis, Missouri. Contact the NPRC in case your ancestor's file was spared, or to request an alternate record verifying your ancestor's service.

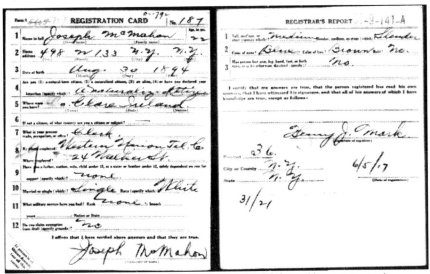

Figure 5. WWI Draft Card for Joseph McMahon. (Ancestry.com)

Rosters show the military organization to which an ancestor was attached, and when. Morning reports show the daily status of an organization. By matching the dates an ancestor was assigned to an organization to its history, you can fill in events on his timeline. Rosters and morning reports are located at the NPRC, but some may be found in published sources. If you want to view the rosters and morning reports this is done in person, and by appointment, at the NPRC Archival Research Room. Alternately, a researcher may be hired to copy them. For more information about these records, see http://www.archives.gov/st-louis/military-personnel/morning-reports-and-unit-rosters.html.

Check your state archives for records or summaries of military service. Some of these records are now available from Ancestry.com.

The National Archives at College Park, Maryland (NARA II) holds military records including unit histories and correspondence.

Information about the times and places of an ancestor's service can be found in special collections and personal papers. You should always look for these collections in archives, libraries and museums. If possible, use online finding aids or contact the reference personnel to search these collections for your ancestor's name or picture. Even if you do not find your ancestor's name in the collections, the materials may provide background about the places and events that your ancestor experienced.

Paperwork was generated when your ancestor was discharged from military service. The discharge document or a final pay voucher may still be in a family member's possession.

I contacted the National Personnel Records Center (NPRC) of NARA by mail to request personnel records for my Grandfathers. I received a call from an archivist asking me to verify some information to confirm that they had the record for the correct Joseph McMahon. I recognized the address in Brooklyn that was given. His records were lost in the 1973 fire, so I received a substitute record, which was a final payment roll record (Figure 6).

Another step in researching my Grandfather's service was writing to the New York State Archives for his service abstract card. This was done via mail before the database became available at Ancestry.com.

If your ancestor sought services from the Department of Veterans Affairs, records were generated. You may request information about a veteran through the Freedom Of Information Act (FOIA) request. See http://www.oprm.va.gov/foia.

Local histories are another great resource for the details of an ancestor's military service. Books may have been written about the soldiers of a county or town. These biographies can provide many details or clues to follow.

Tombstones or obituaries may hold information about military service.

The following chapter discusses finding these records of military service online.

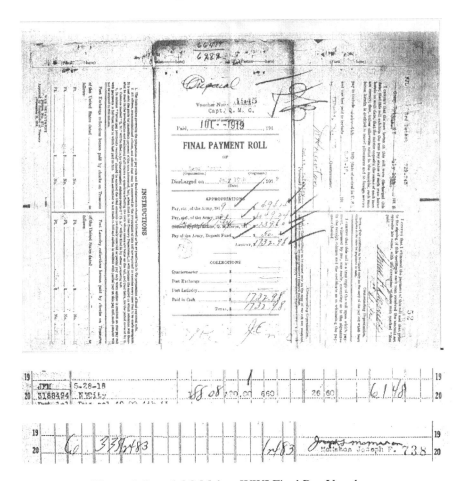

Figure 6. Joseph McMahon WWI Final Pay Voucher.

6 FINDING RECORDS ONLINE

It has been said that online records are like the tip of an iceberg; the majority of records exist offline in various archives, people's homes and other physical locations. The records that we seek lived in the physical world before they entered cyberspace. This chapter focuses on how to find the basic military records that are online at subscription and free websites. Military Records can be found at subscription websites like: Fold3, Ancestry.com, and FamilySearch. Ancestry.com is a subscription website that has a wealth of military records. Fold3 subscription website specializing in military records. FamilySearch is a free website where you may find military records of your ancestors.

Ancestry.com

The records at Ancestry.com may help you determine the branch of your ancestor's military service. At Ancestry.com, you can search on all records, and then filter your results to see only military records. To limit the search so that only results from military record sets are shown, select Military from the Search drop down menu as shown in Figure 7.

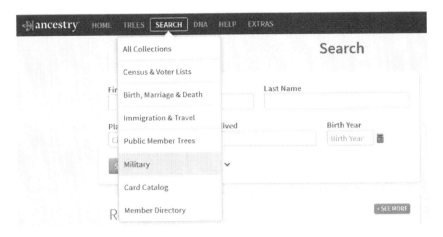

Figure 7. Ancestry.com Military Records Search.

The option I recommend is using the Military Records Landing Page shown in Figure 8.

From this landing page, I have been able to locate records in smaller databases that may not be included in a search through the myriad of databases on Ancestry.com. It is located at: http://www.ancestry.com/cs/us/militaryrecords

Figure 8. Searching Ancestry.com from Military Landing Page.

Fold3

Fold3 is owned by Ancestry.com, but it is not included in a basic Ancestry.com subscription (Figure 9).

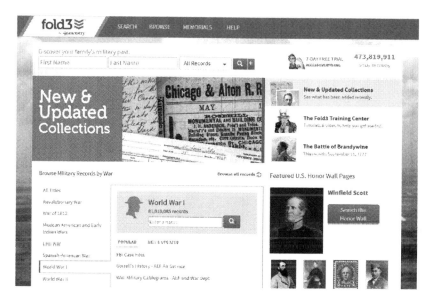

Figure 9. Fold3 Home Page.

Fold3 hosts premium content about World War I and displays free content from other sources. You can search for records by clicking on the Search button at the top of any page. From the Search page, enter a first name and a last name, or select "Advanced Search" to be able to enter more information.

Browsing is another way to access records on Fold3. From the home page select World War I, select options from the menus that are presented to find publications and documents. There are several publications (databases) that may be useful, depending on the state in which your ancestor lived. Databases from the War Department, Naturalization Records of WWI soldiers and records from other countries are available. The Fold3 list of World War I database titles (Figure 10) can be browsed at: https://www.fold3.com/browse/250.

Figure 10. Fold3 WWI Records.

FamilySearch

FamilySearch contains records and transcriptions that can be accessed for free. A search at https://familysearch.org/search will return records in all categories. Use the menu on the left to filter your results by collections. Check the results to see if your search returned any records in the Military category (Figure 11).

Another option for finding records is to use the map on the search page. Click on the United States, and select the ancestor's state from the popup menu. Click on the state name to go to the page for that state where you can search the indexed records by selecting links to view the browsable image-only databases.

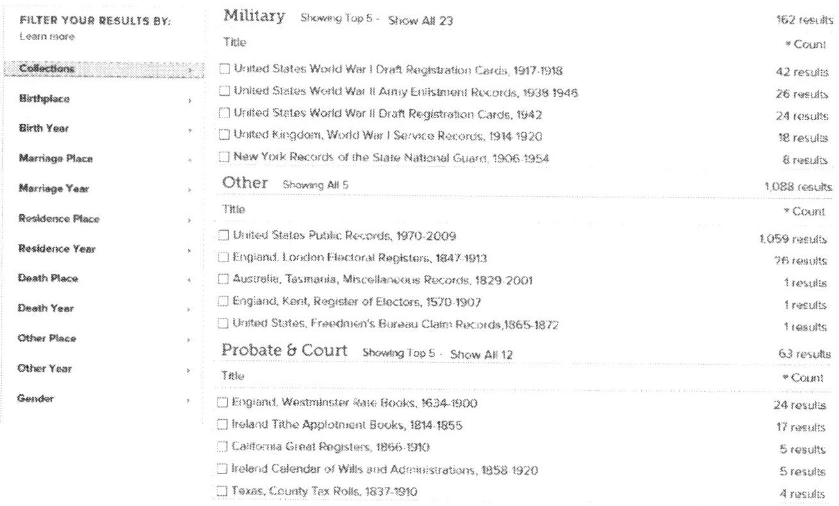

Figure 11. Filtering FamilySearch for Military Records.

7 CEMETERIES

Genealogists certainly know the benefits of cemetery research. In addition to finding names and dates on tombstones, veterans graves may contain facts about their service. The branch of service, rank and military organization may be listed on the tombstone.

Military Cemeteries

If your ancestor is buried in a national cemetery, you can find a listing for his grave and service information in the U.S. Department of Veterans Affairs National Graveside Locator (Figure 12) at: http://gravelocator.cem.va.gov/index.html.

Soldiers who died during the war were buried overseas. The American Battle Monuments Commission (ABMC) operates and maintains 25 American cemeteries and 27 memorials, markers and monuments in 27 countries. The ABMC website can be found at: https://www.abmc.gov (Figure 13). For a veteran's grave information, search at: http://www.abmc.gov/database-search.

To search for only WWI soldiers, uncheck all but the WWI box.

You do not have to fill in all the fields; try a first and last name. For example, to find all the soldiers killed in the Battle of St. Mihiel from New York State without a name select these fields: Entered Service From: New York, Branch of Service: U. S. Army, War Conflict: World War I and Keyword: Mihiel

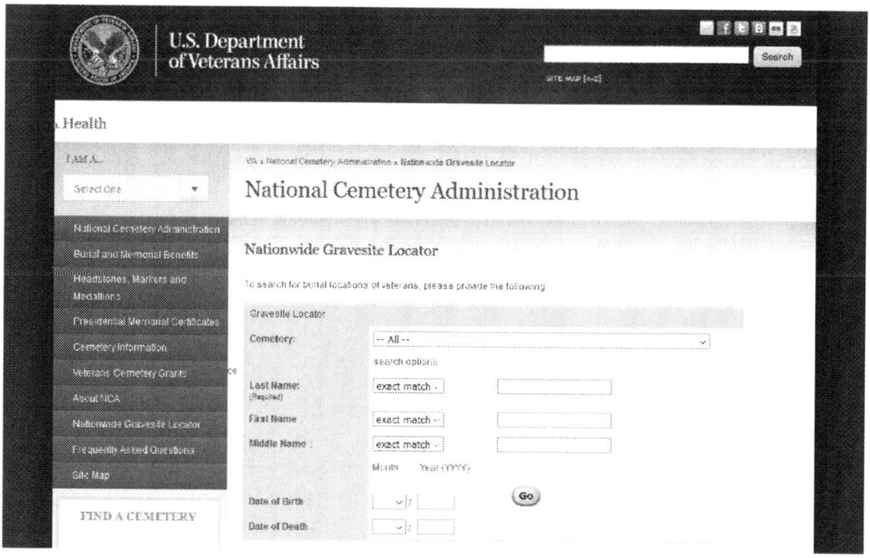

Researching Your U.S. WWI Army Ancestors

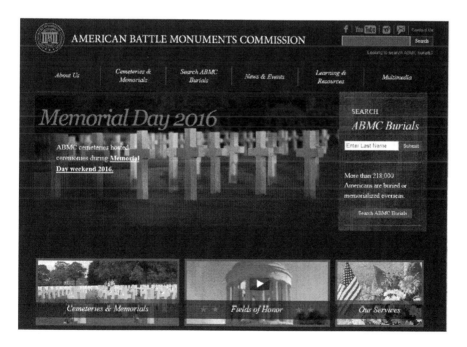

Figure 12. VA National Graveside Locator.

Figure 13. American Battle Monuments Commission Home Page.

The ABMC Commemorative Sites Booklets about the major battles are very informative. From the Cemeteries and Memorial Page at: https://www.abmc.gov/cemeteries-memorials, scroll down to select a link to the Monument or Cemetery. The page for the St. Mihiel Cemetery is shown in Figure 14. The page has links to download the St. Mihiel American Cemetery Visitor Brochure and the ABMC Commemorative Sites Booklet. Maps and a downloadable version of "American Armies and Battlefields in Europe: A History, Guide and Reference Book" can be found at: https://www.abmc.gov/news-events/news/world-war-i-historic-reference-book-now-available-abmcgov. In this book, the Pioneer Infantry Regiments are referred to as Pioneer Troops, so I had to search for the term "pioneer" to view relevant content.

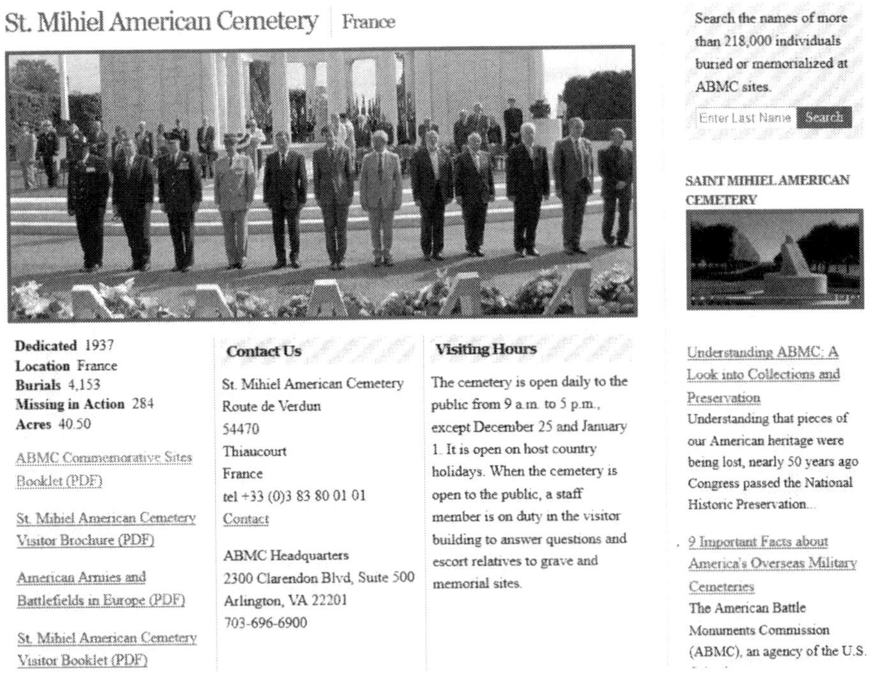

Figure 14. ABMC St. Mihiel Cemetery Web Page.

There are videos about the cemeteries on the ABMC YouTube channel: https://www.youtube.com/user/ABMCVIDEOS.

Findagrave

To search for veterans' graves in non-military cemeteries, use the volunteer website Findagrave, found at: http://findagrave.com. If you find a record of a grave without an image of the tombstone, you can request that a volunteer take a picture of it. If the ancestor's grave is not listed at Findagrave, and you have information that he is buried at that cemetery, follow the steps to add a memorial. After the memorial has been created, you can then request a photo of the tombstone.

Military Tombstones

If a headstone was provided by the government, the application can provide genealogical information. You can search for the application at the database at Ancestry.com, U.S., Headstone Applications for Military Veterans, 1925-1963, found at: http://search.ancestry.com/search/db.aspx?dbid=2375.

FamilySearch

FamilySearch has links to World War I Casualties at: https://familysearch.org/wiki/en/United_States_World_War_I_Casualty_Records. If your ancestor died in WWI, follow the links on that web page to access the books at Google Books as his picture may be printed in them. The books are organized by state. You can also view the books' contents at Ancestry.com.

FamilySearch also has an indexing project for obituaries. Since an obituary can contain information about the deceased's military service, it is worth checking this database. You can search for your ancestor at: https://familysearch.org/obituaries.

8 BATTLES

In spite of their short service during the Great War, Americans participated in many battles. Among them are Chateau Thierry, Belleau Woods (which is important in U. S. Marine Corps history), Marne, Ameins-Oise Offensive, the St. Mihiel Offensive, and Meuse-Argonne Campaign. The Victory Loans poster in Figure 15 reminds Americans of these battles.

For some soldiers, the battles were the defining experiences of their participation in the war. Your soldier may have been injured or killed in these battles. Some U.S. troops in WWI were gassed by the enemy. When you study the battles look for evidence of those injuries.

Participation in a specific battle places your ancestor in a location and time, and includes his actions at that place. Use the information you find to add details to the timeline you are developing.

Much has been written about the battles of WWI. The battles were described in current publications of the time, such as newspapers and magazines. History books were written soon after the war. Over time, they have been revised and joined by other publications. Some of these are discussed in the chapter about books.

Michelin published illustrated guides to the battlefields (1914-1918). One example of these guides is "The Americans in the Great War, Vol II., The Battle of Saint Mihiel (St. Mihiel, Pont-à-Mousson, Metz)" which can be downloaded from Google Books at: https://books.google.com/books?id=uupmAAAAMAAJ.

You will find the stories of the battles tell you much about these day and hours of your soldier's life. Read and study the battles to get perspective about the bigger picture in which your ancestor's service was an important part. You will research from the big picture to the military unit's history to the individual soldier's stories to gain a complete understanding of your soldier's experience.

Military communications contain detailed information about troop movements, assignments and duties.

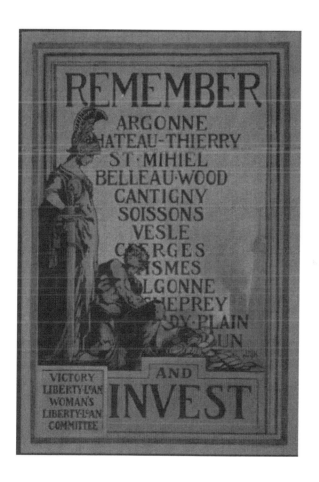

Figure 15. Victory Loans Poster. (Image courtesy of Library of Congress Control Number 2002699399)

The battles of WWI have been analyzed and are still studied in history and military classes. Studies have been published in books and journal publications. They are featured in unpublished manuscripts.

Stories from other soldiers add depth your military ancestor. You may not find any written or oral history that mentions your ancestor's name, but the words of someone who was fighting next to him can put you there on the battlefield. The words of the soldier who fought beside your ancestor can describe the sights, sounds, smells, weather and incoming shells. Soldiers' experiences can be found in published sources, special collections or in military archives. By using these sources, you can become the military biographer of your ancestor.

Maps show the movement of troops, as well as the distances they traveled and terrain they encountered in their marches.

Use the chapters that follow to provide guidance for locating information about the battles in newspapers, photos, books, maps and using NARA and military archives.

9 BOOKS

Books may hold information about your ancestor by name, military unit, or the battles in which he fought. Knowing the military organization in which your ancestor served allows you to locate materials about the places he was stationed, his duties and daily life during the war. Search for books about the military regiments, the Army to which he was attached and his battle participation.

Remember to search for books about World War I, and The Great War. Learning about the history of WWI allows you to put the smaller pieces you find into a larger context.

The battles and history of World War I are still studied. Make sure that you investigate educational resources as well as contemporary publications to further your research.

Google Books

When you locate the title of a book that is out of copyright, you may be able to download it. Search for the title at Google Books (https://books.google.com) in one of the possible formats, or at the Internet Archive (https://archive.org).

A book that you should consult for history and context is the "Battle Participation of Organizations of the American Expeditionary Forces in France, Belgium, and Italy. 1917-1918" (https://books.google.com/books?id=VnHIAAAAMAAJ). In this book you can search for a military organization to see the battles in which your ancestor participated. For example, Figure 16 shows the information on page 48 about the 51st Pioneer Infantry's Battle Participation.

51st Pioneer Infantry:
    (1) St. Mihiel offensive, France, 12 September–16 September, 1918.
    (2) Toul sector, France, 17 September–11 November, 1918.

Figure 16. The Battle Participation of the 51st Pioneer Infantry.

Soldiers may have been transferred between units or they may have been attached to different Regiments, Armies, or even assigned to a military organization of another country. Do not forget to search for books about the larger organization. For example, the 51st Pioneer Infantry was assigned to the 301st Engineers. The book, "The Three Hundred and First Engineers: A History 1917-1919", contains information about the 51st Pioneer Infantry in battle and in training during the Occupation of Germany.

The original World War I era books should be out of copyright and can be downloaded. However, the search results may also include reprinted versions that are in copyright. Remember to check all the results to find the older version.

Internet Archive

In addition to out-of-print books, the Internet Archive also contains music, movies and images (Figure 17). It can be found at: http://archive.org.

The Internet Archive takes snapshots of web pages on the Internet, and the WayBack Machine can be used to access those stored versions of web pages. When a link to a search result or a web page you read about is no longer active, paste the link into the WayBack Machine to look for a stored copy of the page.

Figure 17. The Internet Archive Home Page.

WorldCat

Rather than search each catalog of every library, use the worldwide catalog at WorldCat at: http://www.worldcat.org. Be sure to search WorldCat for the military unit in titles and keywords.

An example WorldCat search for the 51st Pioneer Infantry is shown in Figure 18. By creating a free account, you can save titles in lists. When you find titles of interest, make a note of the location of the book and schedule a visit or arrange an interlibrary loan.

Military History

You can find Army publications and resources about World War I at the U.S. Army Center of Military History website, located at: http://www.history.army.mil/html/bookshelves/resmat/WWI.html, Click on the tabs for Published Material, Archived Material, WWI Images and Special Posting (Figure 19).

Figure 18. Example Search Results in WorldCat.

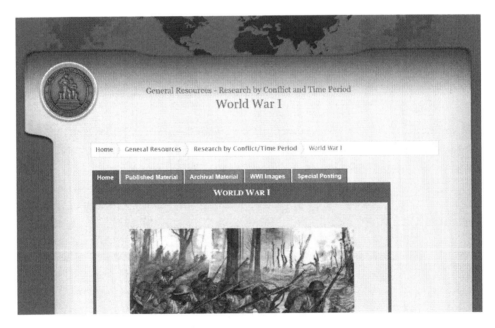

Figure 19. U.S. Army Center of Military History WWI Resources.

10 AMERICAN MEMORY COLLECTION

The American Memory Collection at the Library of Congress is a rich assembly of material that documents the American experience. The collection contains issues of the "Stars and Stripes" military newspaper; recordings of music and speeches; images, posters, photos and text; and sheet music. It is located at: http://memory.loc.gov/ammem/index.html. The Home Page is shown in Figure 20.

Some of the material is directly applicable to developing the timeline and details of military service. Things you find may help give you context. Other items will immerse you in the sights and sounds of the time.

You can search or browse through the collections. By browsing through a specific collection, you can locate materials that might not be located by searching the website.

In the "American Leaders Speak" collection, visit the page with Recordings from World War 1 and the 1920 election at: http://memory.loc.gov/ammem/nfhtml/nfhome.html. From this page you can Search by Keyword, or Browse by Subject or Speaker.

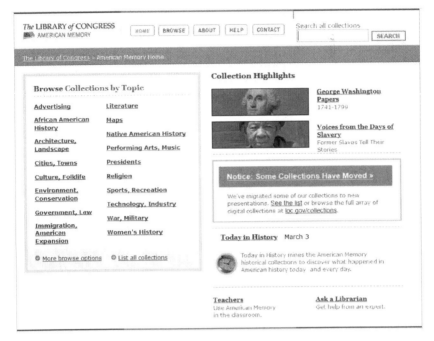

Figure 20. American Memories Collection Home Page.

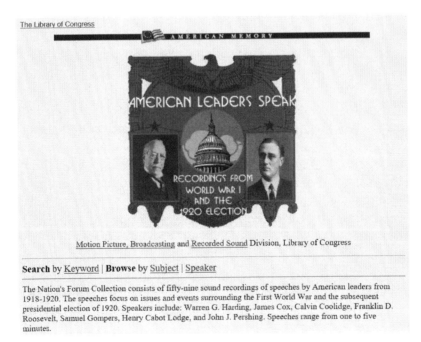

Figure 21. Recordings from WWI and the 1920 Election.

From the list of recordings from WWI and the 1920 Election at: http://memory.loc.gov/ammem/nfhtml/nforSpeakers01.html, you can listen to General J. J. Pershing speak about the battlefields of France (Figure 21). Alternately, you can browse through the Subjects in World War, 1914-1918, that are listed at: http://memory.loc.gov/ammem/nfhtml/nforSubjects01.html.

When I typed "51st Pioneer Infantry" in the search box, shown in Figure 22, there were only two results. Typing "51st Pioneer" yielded more results. The results included articles from "The Stars and Stripes" newspaper (Figure 23).

Figure 22. Search box.

Figure 23. Stars and Stripes Result.

The search results page in "The Stars and Stripes" newspaper collection includes a choice to download the page or the whole issue as a PDF file. Be sure to note the page number and position of the article you found in the list of search results; searching the in downloaded PDF document may give the same results.

You can download sheet music from the era. Among the sheet music that you can download is both "I'm Raising My Boy to Be a Soldier" and "I Didn't Raise My Son to Be a Soldier".

The choice of keywords is important. Keywords are stored with each item, and only those items matching the specific keywords will be returned when searching. Be flexible and remember to try different variations of the keywords in your searches. Although you can try abbreviations, the full words "world war" returned many more results. Remember to try the number '1' and the letter 'I' when searching. For example, searching for keyword containing the letter, "WWI", returned only two results for sheet music. A search using the keyword including a number "WW1" returned no results. In a broader search, "world war 1" (with the number '1') returned over 1300 results while "world war I" (the letter 'I') returned over 1600 results.

Be sure to search the American Memory Collection for your ancestor's military units, to see what you can find. Because this website holds so much material containing the sights and sounds of American lives, remember to search it for all your ancestors' times.

11 MAPS

Building a timeline using the dates and locations for an ancestor's activities is interesting. The timeline is an aid to solving mysteries, but it is only one dimensional. Maps are two dimensional, giving perspective, distances and geography to the events we research. Following the route of troop train through a country, or knowing the terrain through which a soldier marched at night, adds to the understanding of his experience. Maps contain not only troop movements, but also the geographic context of the campaigns.

The United States Military Academy West Point Department of History has an online Campaign Atlas of the Great War (Figure 24) at: http://www.westpoint.edu/history/SitePages/WWI.aspx.

The Library of Congress has a Collection of Military Battles and Campaigns at: https://www.loc.gov/collections/military-battles-and-campaigns. Some maps are drawn, while others are imprinted. Some of the maps are available online, while other entries are only the catalog records. A good place to start is by learning about the collection at: https://www.loc.gov/collections/military-battles-and-campaigns/about-this-collection.

You can browse the maps by Subject (Figure 25). When you browse, you may find interesting items that a direct search might not reveal. The entry for World War maps includes both World War I and World War II. You can continue to refine your search to limit the number of results.

Margaret M. McMahon, Ph.D.

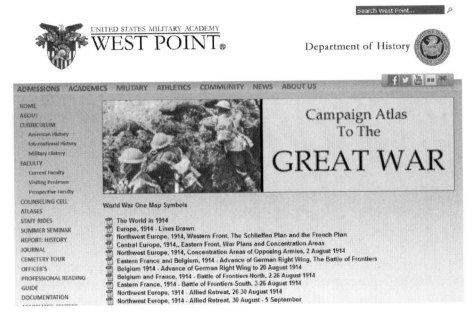

Figure 24. West Point Campaign Atlas to the Great War Web Page.

Subject	
Maps	3,617
United States	3,333
History	1,406
Early Works to 1800	1,262
Virginia	1,206
Civil War	1,183
Maps, Manuscript	944
Campaigns	499
World War	453
Georgia	257
More Subjects »	

Figure 25. LOC Military Battles and Campaigns.

When searching, leave the dropdown menu set to the default "This Collection". You can enter your keyword(s) in the text box (Figure 26). In this case, I used St. Mihiel. While you are on any other page on the Library of Congress website you can select "Maps" from the dropdown menu to limit the search to show only maps in the results.

Figure 26. LOC Military Battles and Campaigns Search Box.

There is a decorative historical map with an overview of the American Expeditionary Forces and border of the combat divisions badges available at: https://www.loc.gov/item/2003627001/#.

Google maps or Google Earth can be useful in mapping an ancestor's locations through the war. Some of the places that are named may no longer exist; when that happens look to older maps from the time period. Google maps can be searched at: https://www.google.com/maps. Google Earth Pro can be downloaded from: https://www.google.com/earth.

Maps for the major battles can be found in historical books, including "American Armies and Battlefields in Europe" at: https://www.abmc.gov/sites/default/files/publications/AABEFINAL_Blue_Book.pdf. Be sure to check on the publication rights before republishing any media.

12 PHOTOS AND VIDEOS

While maps add a second dimension to a timeline, photos add the third dimension to the depth to our understanding. Viewing images of the soldiers, the landmarks and the battlefields offer glimpses into their war that take us back in time. For example, you can combine the photos of a destroyed town that you find during your research with the facts you uncovered about your ancestor using the town's rubble to fill shelled roads as a battle raged around him.

There are also some online videos that may be of interest, including films taken during this war.

Photos: NARA

The National Archives and Records Administration offers photographs both online and at NARA II. Accessing the Photograph Archives at NARA II will be discussed in the next Chapter. Search NARA's catalog for photographs using their Advanced Search page: https://catalog.archives.gov/advancedsearch. For the Type of Archival Material, select "Photographs and Other Graphic Materials" from the dropdown menu (Figure 27).

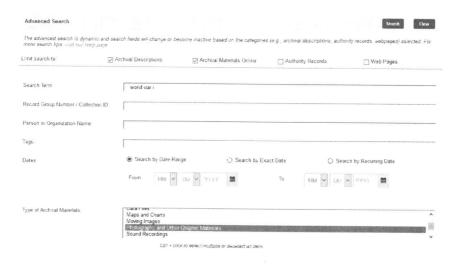

Figure 27. NARA Advanced Search.

Searching using the above settings will return records for images that may or may not be online.

By choosing "JPEG", "TIFF" and/or other image file formats as the File Format of Archival Descriptions, the search will return images that are online. Use the Control key and left click to select multiple options (Figure 28).

Example search results are shown in Figure 29. When viewing the results, you can click forward or backward using the arrows in the Records field to see other images within the results (Figure 30). These images are unrestricted in use.

Figure 28. NARA Advanced Search File Format.

Margaret M. McMahon, Ph.D.

[US Participation in World War I, French Battlefields]
From RG: 286
Photographs of Marshall Plan Programs, Exhibits, and Personnel
National Archives Identifier: 19992528 **Local Identifier:** 286-MP-fra-08377.jpg
Creators: Department of State. Agency for International Development. 1961-10/1/1979; Economic Cooperation Administration. 1948-12/30/1951; Department of State. International Cooperation Administration. 6/30/1955-11/1961; Foreign Operations Administration. 8/1/1953-6/30/1955; Department of State. Technical Cooperation Administration. 9/8/1950-6/1/1953

[US Participation in World War I, French Battlefields]
From RG: 286
Photographs of Marshall Plan Programs, Exhibits, and Personnel
National Archives Identifier: 19992526 **Local Identifier:** 286-MP-fra-08376.jpg
Creators: Department of State. Agency for International Development. 1961-10/1/1979; Economic Cooperation Administration. 1948-12/30/1951; Department of State. International Cooperation Administration. 6/30/1955-11/1961; Foreign Operations Administration. 8/1/1953-6/30/1955; Department of State. Technical Cooperation Administration. 9/8/1950-6/1/1953

[US Participation in World War I, French Battlefields]
From RG: 286
Photographs of Marshall Plan Programs, Exhibits, and Personnel
National Archives Identifier: 19992524 **Local Identifier:** 286-MP-fra-08372.jpg
Creators: Department of State. Agency for International Development. 1961-10/1/1979; Economic Cooperation Administration. 1948-12/30/1951; Department of State. International Cooperation Administration. 6/30/1955-11/1961; Foreign Operations Administration. 8/1/1953-6/30/1955; Department of State. Technical Cooperation Administration. 9/8/1950-6/1/1953

[US Participation in World War I, French Battlefields]
From RG: 286
Photographs of Marshall Plan Programs, Exhibits, and Personnel
National Archives Identifier: 19992522 **Local Identifier:** 286-MP-fra-08371.jpg
Creators: Department of State. Agency for International Development. 1961-10/1/1979; Economic Cooperation Administration. 1948-12/30/1951; Department of State. International Cooperation Administration. 6/30/1955-11/1961; Foreign Operations Administration. 8/1/1953-6/30/1955; Department of State. Technical Cooperation Administration. 9/8/1950-6/1/1953

Figure 29. NARA Photo Search Results.

Figure 30. NARA Photo Result.

The photos I found most interesting were from Record Group 286. The label of this Record Group is "US Participation in World War I, French Battlefields". However, in addition to images of battlefields, there were images of soldiers on trains, on boats, marching, working and training.

Photos: New York Public Library

Photos can be found at library collections (Figure 31). The Miriam and Ira D. Wallach Division of Art, Prints and Photographs: Photography Collection of the New York Public Library offers online images that have no known U.S. copyright restrictions. It can be found at: http://digitalcollections.nypl.org/items.

Figure 31. Troops in a Trench (From the New York Public Library)

Figure 32. Fresnes-en-Woevre, in the St. Mihiel sector (From the Library of Congress Control Number 2007663860).

Photos: Library of Congress

Photographs can be found at the Library of Congress (Figure 32). Search from the Home Page at: https://www.loc.gov. From the dropdown menu select "Photos, Prints, Drawings" and enter keywords in the search box.

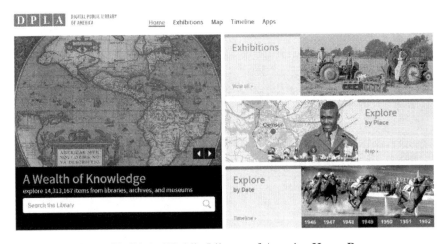

Figure 33. Digital Public Library of America Home Page.

Photos: Digital Public Library of America

The Digital Public Library of America, found at: https://dp.la, is a portal to the digital collections in America's libraries, archives, and museums (Figure 33).

The timeline is a feature to explore. Selecting 1918 returned 9,043,380 from over 2,000 contributing institutions. You can refine results by Subject, Location and other criteria. Click on the line in the timeline to see a snippet of the results.

Searching for "world war i" returned 72,477 results from 542 contributing institutions. A search for "pioneer infantry" gave 89 results from 26 contributing institutions. For this search, many of the pioneer infantry results were from Civil War material.

Photos: Military Archives

Photos can also be in the collections of Military Archives. Finding content in the military archives is covered in the next chapter.

Videos: NARA

NARA has a YouTube channel with preserved and restored videos. Within it is a playlist of World War I and World War II films (https://www.youtube.com/watch?v=9ifDqlRZh70&list=PLugwV CjzrJsWIM3pm2EAxypQnwI9g51Gt). Rather than typing in this long address, begin at webpage for the YouTube NARA channel at: https://www.youtube.com/user/usnationalarchives. Then look at the playlist. As of this publishing, there are 180 videos in this playlist.

The "The St. Mihiel Drive, 1936" World War I video was from the Official films of the Signal Corps of the U.S. Army taken in France (Figure 34). Note: This video does contain images of fallen soldiers.

Figure 34. The St. Mihiel Drive in the NARA YouTube Channel.

Videos: American Battle Monuments Commission

The American Battle Monuments Commission (ABMC) has 130 videos on its YouTube Channel (Figure 35). You can learn about the 25 cemeteries around the world, including video tour of ABMC Cemeteries overseas. The videos can be found at: https://www.youtube.com/user/ABMCVIDEOS.

Videos: The Great War

The videos on the YouTube channel "The Great War", may provide background information for your research (Figure 36) at: https://www.youtube.com/user/TheGreatWar. A good place to begin is with "Welcome! - The Great War Channel 101" to learn about what is on the channel.

The regular episodes follow WWI as it unfolds, a hundred years ago week by week. There are summaries of the episodes to help you catch up. There are also episodes about the prelude to war.

Researching Your U.S. WWI Army Ancestors

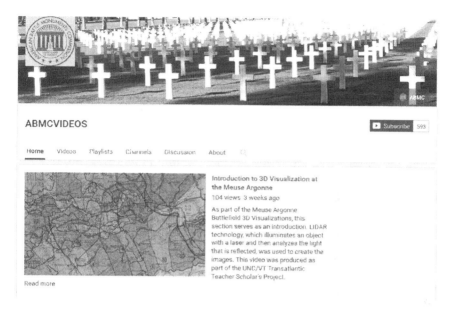

Figure 35. The American Battle Monuments Commission YouTube Channel.

Figure 36. The Great War YouTube Channel.

13 ARCHIVES

Archives can add depth to the narrative you are developing. Although they may not hold items naming your ancestor, there may be materials about the history of your ancestor's service. Some materials may contain the sights and sounds of what your ancestor experienced. The use of archives can transform you into a family historian and a military biographer.

Before visiting an archive, use its online finding aids to get an idea of the materials you will want to access. Also use the website for important information to prepare for your visit. You will want to know the archive's hours of operation; what is and is not allowed in the facility; and if they have a café at the facility. When visiting a location, be clear about the topic(s) you are researching. Be open to suggestions from the archivists and research assistants. They know their collections.

The branches of NARA that will be most useful for researching your WWI ancestor are the military records at NARA II in College Park, MD, and the National Personnel Research Center (NPRC) in St. Louis, MO.

The Army's archives are at the U.S. Army Heritage and Education Center (USAHEC) in Carlisle, PA. USAHEC tells the stories of soldiers through soldier surveys, printed material and photo collections.

This chapter will discuss researching at NARA II and at the USAHEC.

The United States Army Center of Military History has compiled a Master Index of Army Records that lists the types of military records that are available from each war. It can be found at: http://www.history.army.mil/reference/records.htm. Note that many of the links are to the resources you already read about: NARA II at College Park, NPRC, and USAHEC. This activity exists to support Army Staff, Congress, and other federal agencies. It may take years for a reply to a written request from a veteran or the public, but researchers may make an appointment with a staff historian to view working files.

Online Finding Aids

The first step in researching at an archive is to visit its website. Review the online collections for material relevant to your studies. Then, develop a list of items that you want to view. This is invaluable to have a good start to your trip. You will use this list when you contact the staff at the archives to make sure that the records you want to view are available.

Visiting NARA II at College Park

Before I visited, I consulted NARA's online catalog for records about the Pioneer Infantry in WWI. The index to The Records of the American Expeditionary Forces (World War I) (Record Group 120) can be found online at: http://www.archives.gov/research/guide-fed-records/groups/120.html (Figure 37). The term Record Group can also be shown abbreviated as RG.

Upon arriving at NARA II, and passing through a security checkpoint, I received an orientation and was issued a researcher's card. The card doubles as the copy card. After storing extraneous things in a downstairs locker, I went through another checkpoint to access the research rooms. The first time I entered any research room, I had to check in with the people working at the front desk. They directed me how to get started.

In the main research room, the Research Consultation Room was my first stop. In the Research Consultation Room, go to the area under the Military sign.

120.9.4 Records of other tactical units

Textual Records: Records of the 1st-321st Ammunition Trains, 1917-21; 1st-317th Trench Mortar Artillery Batteries, 1917-19; 1st-9th Trench Mortar Artillery Battalions, 1917-19; 30th-64th Artillery Brigades, 1917-19; and 1st-172d Field Artillery Brigades, 1917-19. Records of the 1st Cavalry Brigade, 1917-19. Records of the lst Gas Regiment, 1918-22. Records of Headquarters and Military Police, 1st-322d Division Trains, 1917-19. Records of the 1st-319th Engineer Trains, 1917-19; and 464th-488th Engineer Pontoon Trains, 1918-19. Records of the 1st-192d Infantry Brigades, 1917-19; and 1st-816th Pioneer Infantry Regiments, 1917-19. Records of the 1st-366th Machine Gun Battalions, 1917-20. Records of the 1st and 2d GHQ Military Police Battalions, 1918-19; 122d-134th Battalions, Military Police Corps, 1918-19; and 2d-308th Military Police Companies, 1918-19. Records of miscellaneous quartermaster units, 1918-19, including butchery companies, clothing and bath units, garden service companies and detachments, pack trains, refrigeration units, salvage units, and supply trains. Records of the 1st-622d Field Signal Battalions, 1917-22. Records of the Tank Corps, 1918-19

Figure 37. RG 120 Records mentioning the Pioneer Infantry.

I was interested in learning about the 51st Pioneer Infantry, and brought the timeline cheat sheet shown in Figure 3 with me.

It is important to know that the topic numbers that you find in the online finding aids do not directly correspond with the information to located the actual box on the shelf in the archives. The record topic number needs to be translated to the Stack Area, Row, Compartment and Shelf numbers.

A specialist at the Consultation Room helped me locate the correct binder containing the finding aid to translate that the Record Group to the Stack Area, Row, Compartment and Shelf numbers (Figure 38).

Always discuss your research interest with the specialists. They may suggest other record groups that pertain to your research topic. Always listen to the specialists' suggestions. Even though I went to the Archives in search of RG 120, a specialist recommended that I also consider RG165, which is the "Records of the War Department General and Special Staffs", and showed me the finding aid for that record group.

The Specialist helped me fill out the pull slips that are used for record retrieval. Each pull slip requires the initials of a Specialist before the records can be pulled.

The Specialist also suggested that I go upstairs to the 5th Floor to look for photographs of the 51st Pioneer Infantry while I was waiting for documents to be pulled.

RECORDS OF THE 1ST-6TH, 51ST-65TH, AND 801ST-816TH PIONEER INFANTRY
REGIMENTS. 1917-19. 165 ft.   1255
   Arranged by regiment number; thereunder alphabetically by company
letter, with the records of regimental headquarters first; and thereunder
by type of record. The correspondence is arranged numerically by
assigned number or according to the War Department decimal classification
scheme.

Figure 38. Finding aid for RG 120 Pioneer Infantry records (entry 1255).

Figure 39. Pull slip for RG 120, Boxes 109-129.

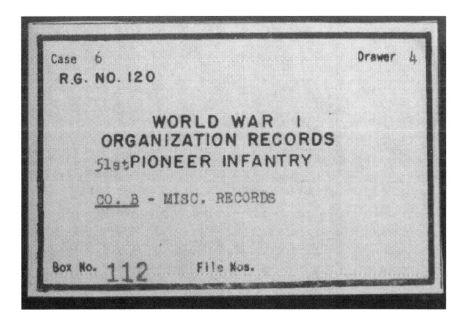

Figure 40. Label on RG 120 Box No. 112.

The initial five boxes from RG 120 contained correspondence of the 51st Infantry Regiment, which is not the same organization as the 51st Pioneer Infantry. So I had to see a specialist and ask how to get the correct records pulled. She had to add additional information to the pull slip (Figure 39). The pulls would take some time, so during the wait I went through the correspondence and documents of the 51st Infantry Regiment. There were some interesting documents, like the price list for items at the YMCA canteens and the rules for soldiers riding trains. The infantry had concerns about equipment and building barns for their horses.

When the correct boxes were pulled, the contents held folders with the books and paperwork for the administration of running the 51st Pioneer Infantry (Figure 40). The contents included the correspondence books that are indexes to the packets of correspondences. The sheathes of paper included requests for discharge; a request for a guitar; Deserters Descriptive cards; requisitions for transportation; telegrams; supply requests; furlough requests; requests for passes; changes to allotment of pay; cancellation of Liberty bonds; property and equipment paperwork; and records of promotions and demotions

These boxes also contained charge sheets for Courts Martial. Among the punishments were fines, hard labor, and forfeiture of pay.

Scanning the Correspondence book of the 51st Pioneer Infantry, I found Joseph McMahon's name. He had been transferred to take part in the IV Corps Vocational School in Mayen, Germany. The first letter was the IV Corps Vocational School acknowledging receipt of his records (letter number 558 dated 16 Apr 1919) and the second letter was about returning his records. (letter number 591 dated 16 May 1919). The correspondence book entry (Figure 41) was useful in locating the letter itself (Figure 42).

RG 165 proved to be a rewarding Record Group. Box 439 held folders containing records for the 51st Pioneer Infantry including: Station Lists, Regiment History, movements, billeting, training and athletics.

591 May 16/19
From: Commandant, IV Corps Voc. School, ...
To: C.O. Co. B 51st Pion. Inf.
Subject: Transfer of Records
1st Sgt. John Mack, 1228127
Pvt 1cl. Joseph F. McMahon 3188494
Pvt James S Hicks, 3184610
Ans 593

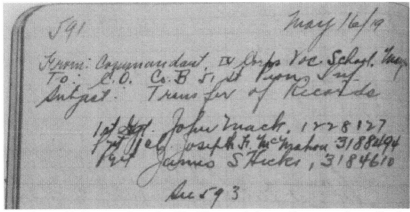

Figure 41. Excerpt from the 51st Pioneer Infantry Correspondence Book.
Declassified Authority No. 903062.

1. Attaching herewith Service Records, Individual Equipment Records and Pay Cards of the following enlisted men returned to you per telegram #1138 - G 4-3 Hq Third Army, Dated May 12, 1919:

1st Sgt. John Mack, #1228127
Pvt 1cl. Joseph F. McMahon, #3188494
Private. James S. Hicks , #3184610

2. Kindly acknowledge receipt of the above records.

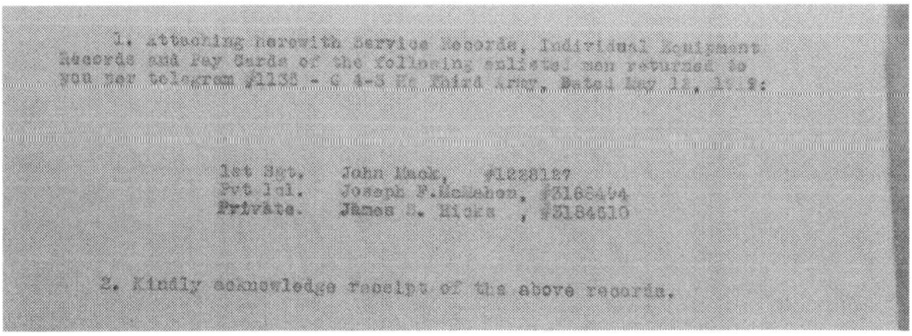

Figure 42. Excerpt from the 51st Pioneer Infantry Correspondence No. 591.
Declassified Authority No. 903062.

Hint: I recommend that you keep a list of the box numbers within the Record Group that you look at, either in a file on your laptop, or using pencil and paper. Keep track of what you find in each relevant folder of each box.

You are required to consult NARA personnel at the copying desk before you use the copiers or take digital photographs of records.

The 5th floor Photograph Room uses an old fashioned card catalog. I asked for and received help finding the one photo related to the 51st Pioneer Infantry. I filled out a pull slip for that photo. When I returned to view the photograph, white cotton gloves were given to me to wear when handling it. The only photo indexed under the 51st Pioneer Infantry was an image with one of its officers, Capt. F. M. Elliott. It was taken on 3/29/1919 of a group of officers who had attended an Arts & Science Course at the University of Edinburgh (Figure 43).

Figure 43. NARA Record Identification 111-SC-898 WWI Number 160146.

State Archives

Another useful archive in your research is the state archives where your ancestor lived. Check the website for that state's archives to find which records or summaries about military service they hold. There may be an index online, or possibly the records themselves. Some of the records may be found on Ancestry.com.

To find your ancestor's state's archives use the list at: http://www.archives.gov/research/alic/reference/state-archives.html.

You can also use the Google search engine to locate the website for your ancestor's State Archives.

Search terms: <state> archives

If the state has two words, use quotation marks around the state's name, as in "New York" archives.

Military Archives

Each branch of the U.S. military has its own archive. The Coast Guard has a genealogical research web page. The web pages for all branches are shown in Table 1. (The U.S. Air Force did not exist during World Wars I and II; it is included because of its collections.)

Table 1. Military Archives Websites.

The U.S. Air Force Historical Research Agency http://www.afhra.af.mil
The U.S. Naval History and Heritage Command Archives http://www.history.navy.mil/research/archives.html
The Archives and Special Collections Branch of the Library of the U.S. Marine Corps http://guides.grc.usmcu.edu/archives
The United States Army Heritage and Education Center http://www.carlisle.army.mil/ahec/index.cfm
The U.S. Coast Guard's Genealogical Research Page http://www.uscg.mil/history/faqs/Genealogy.asp

U.S. Army Heritage and Education Center

The U.S. Army Heritage and Education Center (USAHEC) holds a staggering amount of information that may assist you in your research about U.S. Army ancestors. They may not have an image of your soldier, or papers with your soldier's name, but they may have material from contemporaries that will shed light on your soldier's experience. The Staff is extremely knowledgeable and is available to help you.

USAHEC holds books about military history and Army publications. There are extensive collections of unit histories and photo archives. There are veterans' surveys from the Spanish-American War to the Cold War, and oral histories. Most post-WWII U.S. Army Chiefs of Staff have donated their personal papers to USAHEC. Of interest to you may be the collections of personal papers, pictures, diaries, and letters.

My trip to USAHEC was rewarding. Before the visit, I located items and collections of interest using the online catalog. After locating the material, I contacted the archive by e-mail to ask whether additional information might be available. You can find links to our online tutorials about using USAHEC's online resources at the end of this chapter.

The list of documents I wanted to view were:

1. The 51st pioneers [weekly]
2. The Moses Thisted photograph collection
3. The WWI Veterans Survey Pioneer Infantry documents for SGT John Mansfield
4. The SGT John Mansfield photographs (Photographs from the survey had been transferred to the Photo Archives.)

I sent an e-mail to a Technical Information Specialist to check if these materials would be available on the dates of my visit. As it turned out, Item #4 did need to be cleared for patron use, but it would be before I came.

The Moses Thisted Collection contained only one folder about the 51st Pioneer Infantry. In it was only one picture. The photo is shown in Figure 44. The back of the photo is shown in Figure 45. Moses Thisted was a soldier, an historian and the author of "Pershing's Pioneer Infantry of World War I".

Figure 44. Photo in the Moses Thisted Photograph Collection, Army Heritage and Education Center.

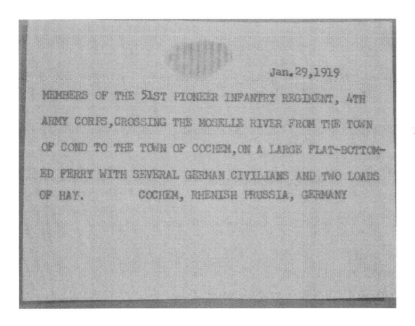

Figure 45. Photo in the Moses Thisted Photograph Collection, Army Heritage and Education Center.

A resource that I found incredibly interesting and helpful to my research into the 51st Pioneer Infantry was the Veterans Survey Pioneer Infantry of SGT Mansfield (Figure 46). He served in Company B along with my Grandfather. This is the closest I can come to learning about my Grandfather's personal war experiences as he left no written or oral memories.

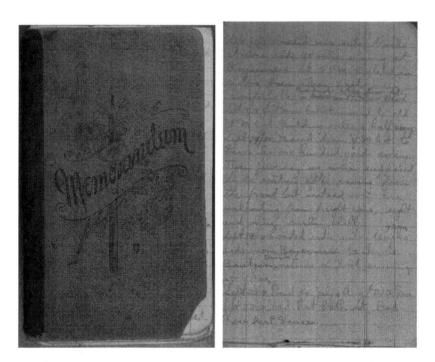

Figure 46. Diary in the WWI Veterans Survey Collection, Army Heritage and Education Center

USAHEC Tutorials on A Week of Genealogy's Blog

The website for A Week of Genealogy hosts many tutorials. Included in them is a set of tutorials about using USAHEC's online resources (Table 2).

Table 2. AWeekOfGenealogy USAHEC Tutorials.

USAHEC: Using the Online Catalog: Reference Bibliographies http://aweekofgenealogy.com/usahec-using-the-online-catalog-reference-bibliographies
USAHEC: Searching the Library and Digital Collections http://aweekofgenealogy.com/usahec-searching-the-library-and-digital-collections
USAHEC: Finding the Veterans Survey Inventories http://aweekofgenealogy.com/usahec-finding-the-veterans-survey-inventories

Contacting An Archive

Your initial contact with an archive is usually by telephoning or e-mailing the Reference Desk. The personnel at the Reference Desk will answer your questions and forward your request to the appropriate Archivist. When the Archivist responds, s/he may ask you for additional data relating to the request. Some records can be copied for free, while others require payment of a fee. Selected records may be available in electronic form and can be sent via e-mail. Some archives require you to visit in person or hire a researcher to view and copy records. Whether you are contacting an archivist remotely or in person, always remember to ask what other material they recommend for the topic you are researching.

14 NEWSPAPERS

Newspapers can be phenomenal sources of information for genealogists. I love to give lectures about using newspapers because of the potential they have for both shedding light on the day-to-day lives of our ancestors and providing a view into the special events of their lives. The use of newspapers takes time and effort to conduct comprehensive searches and suffer through the problems produced by inexact optical character recognition. But give them a try. They contain stories, reports, and personal items about our World War I ancestors.

There are different types of newspapers available. You will be interested in both local newspapers and military newspapers.

Newspapers were published at training bases. Regiments in the army of occupation also published newspapers. The Stars and Stripes newspaper contains articles for the U.S. Armed Forces. Although it is authorized by Congress and the U.S. Department of Defense, it is an independent publication. It was published during the Civil War, and was an eight-page weekly newspaper during World War I. Since World War II, it has been published continuously. See Chapter 10 for more information about The Stars and Stripes newspaper.

This chapter provides a brief overview of what you might find about your WWI ancestor in newspapers. It covers how to find out what newspapers were published in the ancestor's hometown and if those papers might be located online.

Local Newspapers

World War I military ancestors may have been featured in articles in their hometown newspapers. These newspapers may have featured local men when they were inducted, printing lists of names or sometimes pictures. When soldiers wrote home, the news from their letters might appear in the newspaper. Short articles or brief notices in the newspaper might include information about the ancestor including his name, rank, and branch of service. The columns might also carry information about his safe arrival at specific locations. Sad news about a casualty might also appear on the pages.

Keep in mind that while newspapers publish stories about current events, they also run memory and anniversary pieces. After World War I, newspapers would have articles about the reunions of military organizations. A veteran's obituary may also contain information about military service.

Chronicling America

The Chronicling America website (Figure 47) of the Library of Congress will help you find which newspapers were printed in your ancestor's residence during World War I. You can search for newspaper titles by clicking on the "US Newspaper Directory, 1690-Present" button. Click on the "All Digitized Newspapers 1789-1922" to see if the newspaper you seek has been digitized and is available on the website: http://chroniclingamerica.loc.gov.

For more details about using this website, and newspaper research, please see my previous book, "A Week of Genealogy".

NewspaperCat

The Catalog of Digital Historical Newspapers (NewspaperCat) can help you find digitized historical newspapers published in the United States and the Caribbean that are online. NewspaperCat is found at: http://ufdc.ufl.edu/hnccoll (Figure 48).

Margaret M. McMahon, Ph.D.

Figure 47. Chronicling America Home Page.

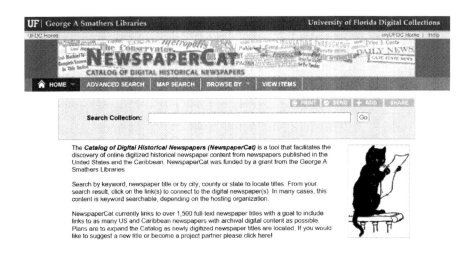

Figure 48. NewspaperCat Home Page.

Fulton Postcards

The Fulton Postcards website contains digitized newspapers from all over the United States and Canada. Many are from New York State. Be sure to read the FAQ_HELP_INDEX to understand how best to search the website. Fulton Postcards is found at: http://fultonhistory.com/Fulton.html (Figure 49).

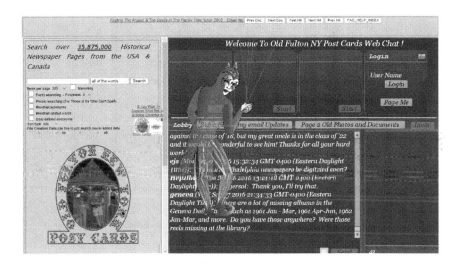

Figure 49. Fulton Postcards Search Page.

Military Newspapers

Seek out military newspapers from World War I. There are newspapers that cover all the military, specific bases and regiments.

The Stars and Stripes newspaper for all the military was covered in the chapter about resources at the Library of Congress.

For those military organizations that trained at Camp Wadsworth in Spartensburg, SC, a camp magazine called the "Gas Attack" was published. Issues of the Gas Attack can be found at: https://dmna.ny.gov/historic/reghist/wwi/infantry/27thInfDiv/Gas_ Attack. Since the website did not have a search engine, I used Google to search the website for articles that contained the 51st Pioneer Infantry.

Google search terms: 51st pioneer site:https://dmna.ny.gov

Look for Regimental newspapers. While serving in the Army of Occupation, the 51st Pioneer Infantry published "Germany's Greatest Newspaper"(Figure 50). It contained news about the Companies of the Regiment, and articles of interest to all the soldiers.

Figure 50. The 51st Pioneers Newspaper.

Check your local library for subscriptions to newspaper databases. Some subscriptions can be used from home with your library card.

15 EPHEMERA

Personal items can flesh out the story of your ancestor's service in World War I. These are the items found in your home and in the homes of your relatives. If you were not lucky enough to inherit any of these items, this chapter will show you where to look for substitutes.

Letters, diaries and personal papers can be found in collections at libraries, at archives and posted on the web. Yard sales and ebay are other places where these items can be found.

Letters

As much as the words in a book can speak to us from the past, a letter can give you a glimpse into the mind of the writer of the letter at the time of its writing. A postcard does combine a short message with a photo, but is usually not as detailed as a letter.

If you do not have access to any letters from your soldier, look for letters from soldiers who served with him. From time to time, letters are for sale on ebay.

The letter in Figure 51 holds a lot of information about the 51st Pioneer Infantry Co. B soldier, Melville Stevens Bulmer, including his time in the Army of Occupation, and his life. Further research revealed that he did become a Minister and did look after soldiers in his ministry. See: https://aweekofgenealogy.com/finding-melville-s-bulmer-in-the-51st-pioneer-infantry-and-beyond.

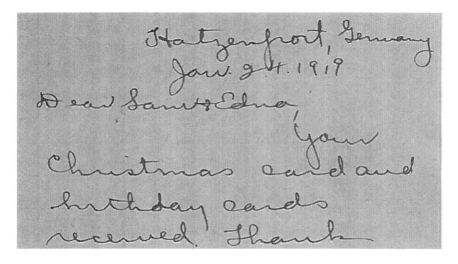

Figure 51. Letter from 51st Pioneer Infantry Soldier (in author's collection).

Hatzenport, Germany
Jan 24, 1919

Dear Sam and Edna,
Your Christmas card and birthday cards received. Thank you very much for your kind remembrances.

It has been very cold here for several days. Yesterday we had our first snow.

The other day I received a pass and visited the city of Coblence [sic]. *It is indeed a wonderful city. It has been my pleasure to visit some of the old castles along the Mosel River. They date back before the time of Christ. Not only these places of interest have I seen but ancient roads, bridges, fortresses built by the Romans which we studied in Ancient History. We walked along the Rhine River and visited the Kaiser Wilhelm Andenkmal* [monument] *It seems strange that on my birthday that I was given leave.*

I have a chance to go to England to finish my theological course. I don't know for sure whether it will come to pass, but I am waiting to hear the word that I can go.

It was just a few days ago that I heard of the death of Joel. I saw it in a Catskill paper that one of the boys had. It was quite a surprise to me. I feel so sorry for Mr. & Mrs. Austin. It sure is a hard blow to them, but it was no harder than the loss of my own Brother. We are in God's keeping.

I am teaching school in the evening for the foreigners and others who can not read and write. It is indeed very interesting work.

Many a time I have turn [sic] my thoughts toward the little village of Cairo as I have been in the thick of the fight; when ordered to do somethings which might have meant my life. But God be thanked I came out safe and sound.

I expect to be home around the first of May perhaps before that – anyway by May first.

We are all in excellent health but anxious to get home. To be sure Cairo shall be my first stop after seeing Mother.

How is the baby. Give my best regards to all my Cairo friends.
With best wishes to all
Yours Most Sincerely,
  Melville

The statue mentioned in the letter may have been the statue of the mounted Emperor William I of Germany, in Koblenz, Germany.

Diaries

Diaries are the personal papers that were kept by the soldier, for his own benefit. Diaries can be found in archives' collections and online
To find personal collections, use finding aids for archives and also WorldCat. You may find that individuals have posted diaries online.
Gordon Van Kleeck, was a private in Company F of the U.S. 51st Pioneer Infantry. His transcribed journal is online at: http://freepages.genealogy.rootsweb.ancestry.com/~treebz65/mom side/vankleeck/gordonvk/gvkjournal/gvkjournalindex.html. Even though he was not in the same company as my Grandfather, the whole Regiment shared many common experiences. His story of crossing the Atlantic Ocean was an example of something all but one of the companies of the 51st Pioneer Infantry Regiment did together.
A web page of links to diaries of soldiers from many countries of

The Great War are at: http://www.war-diary.com/worldwar1.htm. This web page contains links to 32 AEF soldiers.

Fold3 has unit diaries of English WWI War Diaries at: https://blog.fold3.com/uk-wwi-war-diaries.

Dogtags

Dogtags are items that are carried by the soldier during his time in the military. WWI dogtags were circular, while later dogtags are rectangular with rounded edges. You or your relatives may find some dogtags at home. When my cousin asked me to return dogtags she had to the owner's descendants, we found that she also had our Grandfather's dogtag (Figure 52). During World War I he served in the United States. His photo appears on the cover of this book.

Figure 52. World War I Dogtag for A. H. Gilroy.

There are vendors who will create replica dogtags (Figure 53) based on photographs you provide or using your ancestor's information. Search online for this service.

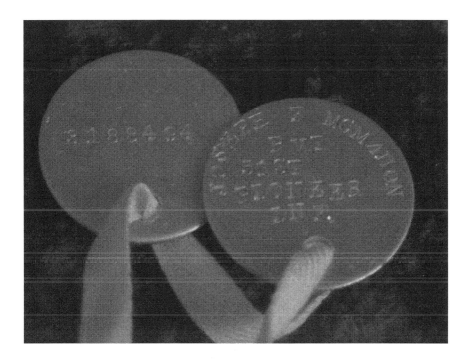

Figure 53. World War I Reproduction Dogtag for Joseph F. McMahon.

Medals

Medals are tangible items that the soldiers would have been able to wear. Medals can be found on ebay, Amazon Marketplace and other online sellers. They can also be found in thrift stores and other similar stores.

The medals that Joseph McMahon would have been entitled to wear are shown in Figure 54.

Figure 54. WWI Victory Medal (top); WWI NY Medal (bottom) (From the author's collection.)

Mementos

Mementos such as leave passes, programs from concerts, and train schedules may fill in the more personal aspects of life in the military. I did find some of these items in the boxes at NARA II. See Chapter 17 to learn about using social networking to find the images and information that people have shared.

Clothing

Although World War I was a century ago, there are still articles of clothing available. Occasionally online sellers will offer helmets and articles of soldiers' clothing. Replicas are also being sold. Without being knowledgeable in this area, the only advice I can offer is to buy from reputable sellers.

ebay

ebay is an Internet yard sale where you can look for memorabilia for sale. There are WWI medals, letters, postcards and more items listed. When you have refined the keywords in a search so that it returns items relevant to your research, set up an ebay alert. Then you will be automatically notified by e-mail when new items are listed that match the search criteria.

Beware that some items are prohibitively priced. Alternately, you may find yourself in a bidding war.

While you may not want to invest large sums of money to purchase items, it is interesting to look at them. Needless to say, the people who post the images own them and you should not use any image in a publication without written permission.

16 MUSEUMS

Military and war museums present artifacts and memorabilia in educational exhibits. Some museums house an archive. Another great resource found at museums are the docents and other knowledgeable personnel.

National WWI Museum

The National WWI Museum and Memorial is located in Kansas City, MO. Their homepage is at: https://www.theworldwar.org (Figure 55).

Military Museums

Each branch of the U.S. military has a museum, except for the U.S. Army. The main military museums are listed below, and several have virtual tours that you can take on the museum website. Several military bases have small museums.

The National Museum of the U.S. Navy is located at the Washington Navy Yard. It can be found on the Internet at: https://www.history.navy.mil/content/history/museums/nmusn.html.

The website for the U.S. Navy and World War I (Figure 56) is at: https://www.history.navy.mil/content/history/museums/nmusn/explore/exhibits/navy-and-world-war-I.html.

Researching Your U.S. WWI Army Ancestors

Figure 55. National World War I Museum and Memorial.

Figure 56. The U.S. Navy and World War I Website.

The National Museum of the U.S. Marine Corps is in Triangle, VA, outside the gates of the Marine Corps Base Quantico. The website is: http://www.usmcmuseum.com.

The U.S.M.C. World War I web page (Figure 57) can be found at: http://www.usmcmuseum.com/world-war-i.html.

Figure 57. The National Museum of the U.S. Marine Corps World War I Web Page.

The website for the National Museum of the U.S. Air Force is at: http://www.nationalmuseum.af.mil/Home.aspx. The collection for the centennial of World War I (Figure 58) can be found at: http://www.nationalmuseum.af.mil/Collections/Research/WW100.aspx.

The U.S. Coast Guard Museum is located in New London, Connecticut, on the grounds of the Coast Guard Academy (Figure 59). The website is at: https://www.uscg.mil/hq/cg092/museum.

Figure 58. U.S. Air Force World War 1 Centenary Celebration Web Page.

Figure 59. U.S. Coast Guard Museum Website.

The Coast Guard Heritage Museum is located in Barnstable Village on Cape Cod, MA. Their website can be found at: http://www.coastguardheritagemuseum.org.

Currently, the U.S. Army does not have a national museum. Their National Army Museum is under construction at Fort Belvoir, VA. Their website features interactive online exhibits and can be found at: http://thenmusa.org/index.php.

To learn about the U.S. Army, you can visit the U.S. Army Heritage & Education Center (USAHEC) in Carlisle, PA. You can learn more about the collections, visitor activities, the special events they host and their other online resources at their website: http://www.carlisle.army.mil/ahec/index.cfm.

Located at the same facility as the Army Archives is the Soldier Experience Gallery (Figure 60 and Figure 61) and the Army Heritage Trail.

Figure 60. Exhibit in the Soldier Experience Gallery, USAHEC. (Author's photo.)

Figure 61. WWI Exhibit in the Soldier Experience Gallery, USAHEC. (Author's photo.)

One of the exhibits displayed a medal issued by Saint-Mihiel, France, in 1937 to commemorate the WWI battle there (Figure 62).

Figure 62. Exhibit in the Soldier Experience Gallery, USAHEC. (Author's photo.)

The Army Heritage Trail contains outdoor exhibits where you can immerse yourself in almost all U.S. conflicts. To view information about the Trail, and images from the exhibits, see: http://www.carlisle.army.mil/ahec/trail/aht.cfm.

The World War I exhibits include a German pillbox that you can enter (Figure 63).

You can walk through a representative system of Allied Expeditionary Force (AEF) trenches. As you travel through the trenches you can see what life for a soldier was like, and visit the aid station and a headquarters. An entrance to the trench is shown in Figure 64. Figure 65 shows a length of the trench.

Figure 63. Army Heritage Trail German Pillbox. (Author's photo.)

Figure 64. Entrance to Army Heritage Trail Trench. (Author's photo.).

Margaret M. McMahon, Ph.D.

Figure 65. Army Heritage Trail Trench. (Author's photo.)

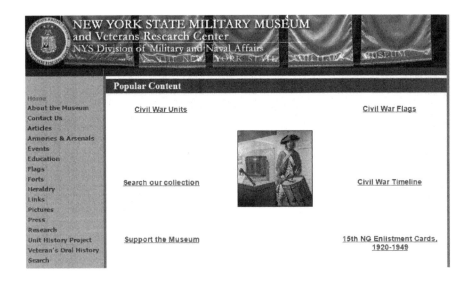

Figure 66. New York State Military Museum Home Page.

State Military Museums

Use Google or another internet search engine to locate websites for State military museums. States may have a physical museum, or a web-only presence. Insert the name of your state where <state> appears.
Keywords: <state> military museum

Remember to look not only for your ancestor, but for information about the places and times that he served. Letters from or pictures of contemporaries may shed light on your ancestor's experiences. (This approach might help you when you search the websites of any museum.)

Example: New York State Military Museum

The New York State Military Museum and Veterans Research Center is part of the New York State Division of Military and Naval Affairs (DMNA) (Figure 66). It is located in Saratoga Springs, NY, and its website is at: https://dmna.ny.gov/historic/mil-hist.htm.

A good starting place on the website is "About the Museum". Here you can learn about the holdings of the museum, as well as its location and hours. Key information is that you have to send your research inquiries by mail, as they do not have the staff to handle telephone requests. I clicked on the "Unit History Project" on the left, then I clicked on "World War One", to see which unit histories are held in their collection, and available online. This web page has links to articles about WWI (Figure 67).

You can search the museum's website by clicking on the search button on the left side of the web page, or navigating to: https://dmna.ny.gov/historic/search (Figure 68). There is a choice of topics to search. To search everything except the roster database, select Search everything.

Margaret M. McMahon, Ph.D.

New York World War One Units

Please Select Unit Type
Artillery | Cavalry | Infantry | Other

New Yorkers who died in World War One

Arvhival Collection: Letters Home from Otilia D. Noeckel
Otilia Noeckel was born June 11, 1890. These letters were sent home to her mother and sisters Mary, Louise, Rose, Emma"Em", and Laura and her brother, W i l l , during the last part of World War I. Otilia was stationed in France for nine months, from November, 1918 through July, 1919.

Article: Black Americans in the US Military: World War One

Article: 1916 State Mobilization camps, by Fred Greguras

Article: The GJG and the New York Guard by SPC Marianne De Angelis, Historical NCO, New York Guard

Manuscript: Was there such a thing in the World's Great War as the Lost Battalion? by Walter J. Baldwin

Manuscript: I was one of the Lost Battalion by Ralph Edmund John(?)

World War One Serviceman Glossary - Common abbreviations used during the war. Provided by Washington State Archives - Digital Archives

Figure 67. New York State Military Museum WWI Units.

NEW YORK STATE MILITARY MUSEUM
and Veterans Research Center
NYS Division of Military and Naval Affairs

Search Everything

AND ▼ KEYWORDS [   ] Use this box to search for names, places, or other subjects.

AND ▼ UNIT [   ] Enter unit numbers here. Use terms like: 1st, 13th, or 165th.

AND ▼ CONFLICT [   ] Enter the name of the conflict here. Library of Congress Subject Headings are used.
For best results use the following:

CONFLICT	USE:
Revolution	1783
Civil War	Civil War
Spanish-American War	1898
WW1	1914
WW2	1945
Korea	Korean
Vietnam	Vietnam

Hints: army / guard - finds records with either word
navy & army - finds records with both words
comput* - finds computer, computation, etc.

Two words typed together will only find records with those two words in that order.

An example: entering
20th / 80th in the UNIT BOX and
Civil War in the CONFLICT BOX will
find all records of either the 20th or 80th regiments during the Civil War

Figure 68. New York State Military Museum Search.

Be flexible when choosing your keyword search terms. Try various combinations, adding and subtracting terms for different searches.

Searching for Keywords: Joseph McMahon gave no results. Searching for Unit: 51st and Conflict: WW1 gave no results. So, I searched for Unit: 51st. The results included World War, 1914-1918 United States. Army; World War, 1914-1918, and Pioneer Infantry, 51st (1917-1919). The results also included New York Infantry 51st Regiment in the Civil War. There were several interesting results, including photographs of the 51st Pioneer Infantry. Remember that you are looking for your ancestor, and also for pictures about the times where and when he served.

This Museum asked that queries be sent via postal mail. When I contacted the Museum to ask about the pictures in the search results, I learned that they had been scanned, but not yet loaded onto the web server.

Other Museums

Check your local museums, the museums near where your soldier ancestor lived, or museums you find in your travels. For example, our family enjoys aviation museums, and in our visits we have found exhibits connected to World War I history.

Contacting Museums

You can always visit a museum's website to learn about its collections and exhibits, and what archives it might have. Remember that some museums are understaffed and underfunded.

Be sure to follow the museum's instructions for requesting information. They may have policies regarding receiving phone calls, e-mail or by mail. Remember to make contributions as you see appropriate.

17 SOCIAL NETWORKING

Social networking is a way to expand your search for materials that other people have or know about. Think of it as a natural extension to looking through the homes of relatives for artifacts. Through social networking you can connect with people who have similar interests and possibly have posted stories, pictures and knowledge to share. This chapter will cover the use of Facebook, Message Boards, and Twitter.

Facebook

There are many Facebook pages and groups dedicated to World War I and military regiments. Search for them using the Facebook search box. In these groups you may find knowledgeable people who can answer your questions.

A Facebook page is like a timeline; anyone can "like" that page. Facebook groups are about forming a community that can share discussions, videos, photos, and documents. A group on Facebook can be public, closed or secret. Since secret groups will not show up in searches, you have to be invited to join them. For public and private groups, you have to ask to join them and a group administrator will grant or deny access. The discussions in a public group are visible to everyone, where only those who are members of a closed group can see the discussions. You must be a member to post and comment in a group.

Researching Your U.S. WWI Army Ancestors

Figure 69 shows the Facebook Page for the 51st Pioneer Infantry, located at: https://www.facebook.com/51stPioneerInfantry.

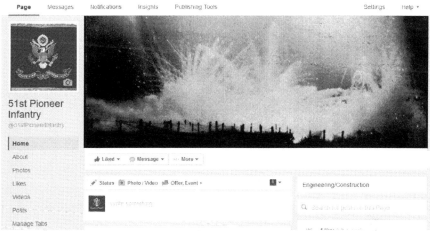

Figure 69. 51st Pioneer Infantry Regiment Facebook Page.

The 51st Pioneer Infantry was assigned to the Third Army during the post-War War I Occupation of Germany. The Facebook group for the Third Army is an interesting community where you can learn more about what the soldiers did during the Occupation (Figure 70). The group is active and contains photos of people and images of items like concert programs.

Figure 70. 3rd Army WWI Facebook Group.

If you cannot find a Facebook page, consider creating one to share information about your soldier's military organization. Post what you learn, and invite others to do the same in the timeline. If the military organization is popular, consider forming a group as a meeting place for other interested people, where group members can exchange content.

A helpful feature is that you can search pages or groups to find specific posts.

Message Boards

Reading and making posts in Message Boards may help you find answers to your questions, or connect with people who have them. Message boards can be used to find information about an organization's service, ask questions, and find out resources. Remember to search these message boards for your topics.

There are genealogical message boards, with the most popular being the Ancestry.com/Rootsweb Message Boards found at: http://boards.ancestry.com. There are several boards within the World War I Topic (Figure 71) that discuss soldiers, divisions and troops at: http://boards.rootsweb.com/topics.Military.wwi/mb.ashx.

Another message board that might help you in your research is the U.S. Militaria Forum at: http://www.usmilitariaforum.com.

A message board that helped me was All Experts Military History, located at: http://en.allexperts.com/q/Military-History-669. When using Google, I located a post on the All Experts Message Boards about the 51st Pioneer Infantry. One of the replies discussed details of the battles and awards that were granted to the 51st Pioneers. The reply mentioned the book "The Battle Participation of the American Expeditionary Forces". I located that book on Google Books and was able to download the book in its entirety in a PDF document.

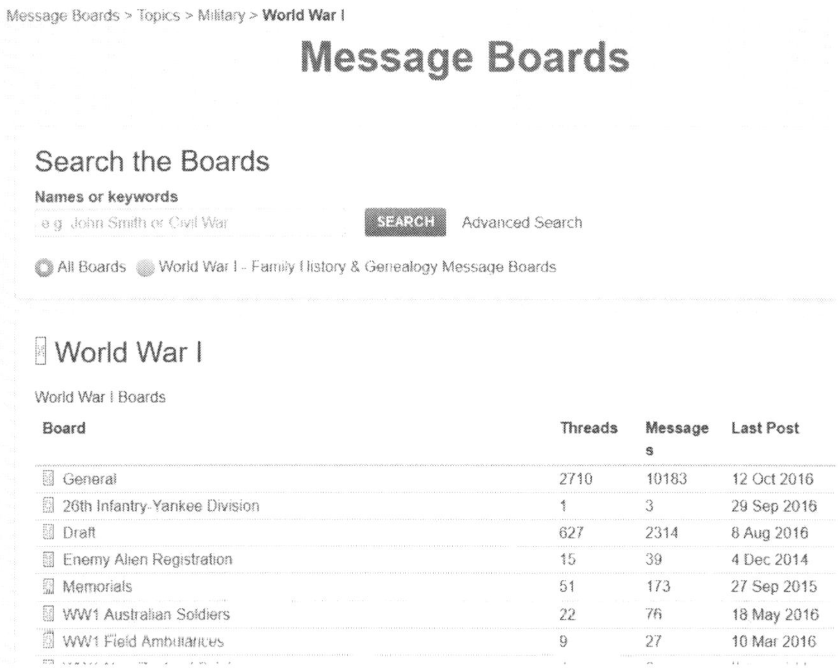

Figure 71. Ancestry.com/Rootsweb World War I Message Boards.

Twitter

Twitter is a social networking platform found at: https://twitter.com (Figure 72). It is free to register and easy to sign up for an account on Twitter. For a new account, you will need to enter a name, e-mail address and password.

Messages in Twitter are called tweets. A tweet is limited to 140 characters or less. Message senders can include a hashtag (#) followed by a searchable term. A tweet with a hashtag will show in the results when others search for the hashtag and term. Use the @ symbol and the username to direct a comment to another user on Twitter.

In Twitter, the search results for #wwi are shown in Figure 73. These results may have images or links that lead you to more content.

Be sure to search for hashtags about the military organizations and history of your WWI ancestor. Try searching for other hashtags like #ww1, #worldwar1.

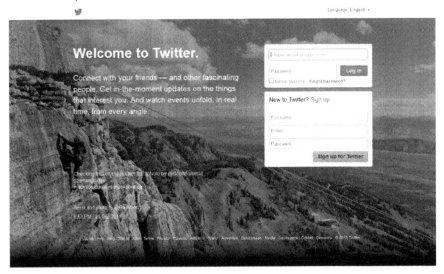

Figure 72. Twitter Home Page.

Figure 73. Search Results for #wwi.

18 PUTTING IT ALL TOGETHER

The techniques and tactics used in previous chapters may have provided you interesting insights into your WWI ancestor. Hopefully, as you made discoveries, you included the information in a timeline for your ancestor. But there is more that you can do to enjoy the material and share it with others in your family. By putting the material into the hands of your relatives, you can get them interested in genealogy. There is nothing better to inspire children who are studying history than to show them how their ancestors were part of the story. These stories make history personal, and make the events jump off the dry pages of a history book to become tales about people from your family.

Enhanced Timeline

During your research you put together a timeline. Consider creating an enhanced timeline that combines the dates and places in the timeline with images and narrative.

While you are searching for information, you will probably collect images relevant to your soldier's experience. You can also find images of ships, towns, battlefields and locations using the websites discussed in Chapter 13. Remember to keep track of the rights for the images you collect, and publish only the material that can lawfully be used.

The enhanced timeline can be very engaging for the non-genealogists who view your work. Involving others is rewarding; they may want to assist you with further research.

Write

A written product can be as simple as an enhanced timeline or as complicated as writing a book. You may consider distributing your written products in an electronic format.

Many word processing programs will allow you to save the document in a portable document format (PDF). A PDF document can be shared easily and opened by any recipient in your family.

You may have collected enough data and have the interest in writing and publishing a book. It will take time to organize and write a book, but it will provide a comprehensive story to the other descendants. Consider donating a copy of the book to a local historical society or library for others to use in their research.

You may want to capture your work a blog. A blog allows the work to be read by anyone with a connection to the Internet. Alternately, you can make a private blog that is accessible by those who have the password. A blog lets you tell the story in bite-sized chunks. It is very quick and easy to get started using one of the two largest platforms, Google Blogger and WordPress.

Hint: Remember to cite the sources of the material that you use!

Scrapbook

A scrapbook is a way to combine the image and text elements of your ancestor's war story in a visual manner. Since we have no stories from my Grandfather, I think of this as the scrapbook he may have made of his experiences.

One option is to create this scrapbook in a document on your computer so that it can shared electronically or printed out.

Presentation

A presentation can be oral, visual or electronic. Consider giving a talk to family at a reunion or other venue, in a story-telling session. Unless you have a great memory, jot down your main thoughts on index cards, or on paper as an outline. You can also use software such as Microsoft PowerPoint to create a shareable multimedia presentation.

Write A Short Summary

Writing engages a different part of the brain than reading does, which adds to the immersion experience. The more parts of the brain we can engage in solving a problem, the better chance we have to get to a solution. Write summaries of the information you find. Compiling lists "by the numbers", of top websites, or short texts are pieces that can be shared. These short products can be shared in e-mails or in blog posts.

The following are examples of this short pieces that I wrote about the St. Mihiel Offensive and published on my blog. On a blog, links can be embedded in the text so that a reader can click on them to visit the websites. Below, the links are shown in parentheses.

St. Mihiel by the Numbers

- 1st Time American Expeditionary Forces were under American Command
- 1st Use of the term D-Day
- 7 American Divisions Advanced at 5 A.M. on 12 Sept 1918
- 1 million artillery shells were fired in the first 4 hours
- 1476 allied air planes participated in the greatest air battle of the Great War
- 16,000 Prisoners were taken in two days

5 WWI St. Mihiel Web Resources:

1. St. Mihiel Drive 1918 United States Army, World War I from the Official films of the Signal Corps of the U.S. Army taken in France. Note: This video does contain images of fallen soldiers. (https://www.youtube.com/watch?v=aHl9AcUiGQE)

2. Pershing's Description of the Battle of Saint Mihiel [Excerpted from the Final Report of Gen. John J. Pershing (Washington, D.C.: Government Printing Office, 1919), pp. 38-43] (http://www.shsu.edu/~his_ncp/Pershing.html)
3. American Expeditionary Force at St. Mihiel (http://www.usaww1.com/American-Expeditionary-Force/American-Expeditionary-Force-St-Mihiel.php4)
4. The Library of Congress American Memories, Today in History: September 12 Saint-Mihiel Offensive (https://memory.loc.gov/ammem/today/sep12.html)
5. "The War with Germany A Statistical Summary" by Leonard P. Ayres, Colonel, General Staff, Washington Government Printing Office, 1919, Chapter VIII. Two Hundred Days of Battle. (http://net.lib.byu.edu/estu/wwi/memoir/docs/statistics/stats8on.htm)

The St. Mihiel Offensive and the 51st Pioneer Infantry

General Pershing's American Expeditionary Force (AEF) launched the Saint-Mihiel offensive. This was the AEF's first independent offensive, with an American Army under American command. The goal was to cut off the rail lines between Paris and the Eastern Front. The St. Mihiel salient was a fortified bulge into France that was 15 miles on either side of St. Mihiel, 20 miles south of Verdun.

The 51st Pioneer Infantry was divided. My Grandfather's Company, B, was attached to First Division. They had their first experience with exploding shells, enemy machine guns and airplanes dropping bombs. The Pioneers kept roads and bridges repaired and rebuilt. They were tasked with keeping the lines of communication open. Trucks were filled with broken brick and stone from destroyed cities and villages, and were prepositioned where enemy attacks were expected. As soon as a shell exploded in a road, a Pioneer crew came and repaired it.

19 TO FRANCE AND BACK

Transporting troops to and from France was a major effort. The trip across the Atlantic Ocean was fraught with danger from attacking German ships and submarines. Everyone had to participate in keeping watch during the days and nights. Putting together the story of the ships and trips in Joseph McMahon's overseas journeys was an interesting and educational activity. This chapter contains the story of those journeys.

You can put together the story of your soldier's trip overseas and back using the resources in previous chapters and photos from the Navy History & Heritage Command.

Anchor's Aweigh: Getting the 51st Pioneer Infantry to France and Back

The history of the 51st Pioneer Infantry included information about the ships that brought Joseph McMahon to France and back home again. Gathering images and more information about these ships fleshes out the details of his WWI service.

From U.S. to Brest, France

On 29 July 1918 the 51st Pioneer Infantry left Camp Merritt, NJ, and marched to Alpine Landing. From there they were placed on ferries to Hoboken, NJ. Then they boarded the steamer USS

Kroonland. On 8 Aug 1918 the U.S.S. Kroonland arrived in Brest, France in the rain.

The U.S.S. Kroonland brought troops to France six times. She also made postwar trips, then was returned to International Mercantile Marine Company.

The journal of Gordon Van Kleeck, a private in Company F of the U.S. 51st Pioneer Infantry, includes the story of the crossing. The soldiers wore overalls rather than uniforms, and sat in the lifeboats during the early morning until sunrise in case there was a submarine attack. You can read Pvt. Van Kleeck's journal at: http://freepages.genealogy.rootsweb.ancestry.com/~treebz65/momside/vankleeck/gordonvk/gvkjournal/gvkjournalindex.html.

Brest was the location of the American Naval Headquarters in France. More than 30 destroyers and multiple yachts escorted the troop and supply convoys that were based at Brest.

While the Kroonland sailed past St. Mathieu lighthouse through LeGoulet Channel into Bay of Brest, French and British airplanes flew low looking for submarines. Several lighter-than-air blimp ships flew low in front of the convoy. The image in Figure 74 shows the U.S.S. Kroonland at the New York Navy Yard, on 24 July 1918, just before its trip to bring the 51st to France. It is painted in "dazzle" camouflage.

Dazzle camouflage patterns were painted on the ships in grey, black and blue. They were effective at distorting a ship's silhouette and making it harder for the enemy to estimate a ship's type, size, speed, and heading. In Figure 75, an airship escorts a convoy into Brest Harbor in 1918. The landing at Brest, France, 8 August 1919 is shown in Figure 76.

Figure 74. U.S.S. Kroonland. Photo courtesy of U.S. Navy, photo NH 52093, Source: Naval History & Heritage Command (NHHC).

Figure 75. Airship Escorts A Convoy into Brest Harbor. Photo courtesy of U.S. Navy photo NH 121616. Source: Naval History & Heritage Command (NHHC).

Figure 76. Landing at Brest, France. Photo courtesy of U.S. Navy photo NH 965. Source: Naval History & Heritage Command (NHHC).

Figure 77. U.S.S. Wilhelmina. Photo courtesy of U.S. Navy photo NH 47885. Source: Naval History & Heritage Command (NHHC).

From St. Nazaire, France to the United States

On 23 June 1919 the 51st Pioneer Infantry sailed from St. Nazaire on the U.S.S. Wilhelmina Figure 77.

On 3 July 1919 they arrived in New York harbor. After the Armistice she made 7 round trips to return the American Expeditionary Force (AEF) troops from France. She was decommissioned on or after 6 Aug 1919 and on 16 Aug 1919 she was returned to the Matson Navigation Company. She originally carried passengers and cargo between the west coast of the US and Hawaii, and after WWI she returned to that service. Later, she was purchased by a British shipping company and was sunk by a U-boat in 1940 while in a convoy between Nova Scotia and Liverpool.

The USS Wilhelmina is shown in front of a coaling facility at the New York Navy Yard on 1 May 1918, painted in dazzle camouflage.

20 GOOGLE

This chapter discusses material I found using one additional tool: Google.

During the process, Google was an invaluable aid to learn about military terms, find publications, learn about locations and locate videos about WWI. Google Maps helped to pinpoint locations listed in the Station List and mentioned in the diaries.

Searching Google for: 51st pioneer infantry has returned good information. The Google search results yielded a website for Camp Wadsworth, Spartanburg, SC. This website includes pictures of the camp and information about the military training there. Some of the information at the website included that the 51st Pioneer Infantry was Formerly 10th New York Infantry, and that it was composed of 39 officers and 904 enlisted men after the reorganization. It was commanded by Colonel J. Guy Deming and filled to wartime strength with draftees. The regiment left Camp Wadsworth on July 17th with 3545 officers and men.

I used Google to locate the New York Military History Museum, which had a lot of online information. Google led me to websites like World War1.com (http://www.worldwar1.com) and the Doughboy Center (http://www.worldwar1.com/dbc/index.htm) where you can learn more about the American Expeditionary Forces.

To learn more about the history the 51st Pioneer Infantry from New York State in World War I, and the contemporary history, my next stop was Google Books.

When you search for content on the Internet, use multiple strategies and multiple search engines.

For those wanting to learn more about how to search for online resources, my book, "A Weekend of Genealogy" covers Googling and Internet searching in depth.

21 CONCLUDING THOUGHTS

This book has outlined the approach I used to research my Grandfather's military service, and the context of his service.

The idea for this book originated during my first visit to the U.S. Army Heritage & Education Center to attend a lecture about using their archives. At that point, I did not know much about the 51st Pioneer Infantry from New York. I was still trying to find out what the term "Pioneer" meant.

This visit, combined with the centennial of the U.S. involvement in World War I, sent me on the path to the research presented here. It would be a year before I was able to return to USAHEC to see the materials in person. The trip was well worth the wait.

There was a lot to learn at the beginning of this journey. My career had led me to work for the U.S. Navy and with the U.S. Air Force; I had little experience with the U.S. Army and its operation.

The journey guided me to better know about a year in my Grandfather's life. His story was set against the world's largest conflict to date, at a time when modern and old technologies were both an essential part of making war. He was part of the first American led offensive. He saw the horrors of destroyed towns. He slept and worked in their ruins. When he traveled into Germany during the occupation, he saw a place that seemed untouched by the war. I learned some of the stories that he would have told his children, and that they would have told us. He now rests below his military tombstone, having traveled there and back to risk it all for his adopted country (Figure 78).

Figure 78. Grave of Pfc Joseph F. McMahon (Photo courtesy of JP Rayder).

As the research progressed, I wrote this book to be the reference that would have helped me at the beginning of the process. As with my other books, I have no doubt that this will be a valuable reference that I will use. Hopefully it will be as valuable to you. Good luck on your journey to learn about your World War I U.S. Army Ancestor.

Margaret M. McMahon, Ph.D.

THE PIONEERS

We read about the doughboys and their valor, which is true,
And of the gallant part they played for the old Red, White, And Blue:
We read about the H.F. A. and their ever-roaring guns,
Also the heavy part they played in blowing up the Huns;
The Infantry, the Cavalry, the hardy Engineers,
But we never read a single word about "The Pioneers".

They slept in pup tents in the cold and worked in mud and mire,
They filled up shell holes in the roads, 'most always under fire;
Far o'er the lines the scout plane goes, directing the barrage,
Just as zero hour draws nigh, or just before the charge.
As o'er the top the doughboy goes, to put the Hun to tears,
But who went out and cut the wire? "The Husky Pioneers."

They buried beaucoup horses and carried beaucoup shells.
From every dump on every front, the kind of work that tells.
A heavy pack on every back, on every track in France,
They never wore the "Croix de Guerre"- They never had a chance.
And as the heavy trucks rolled by, they worked to calm their fears.
Who made the rocky roads so smooth? "The same old Pioneers."

Each branch deserves much credit, and I like to read their praise,
We helped them all, both great and small, in many different ways;
The Shock Troops and brave Marines, the Ammunition Train,
The Signal Corps, the Tank Corps, and the Observation Plane.
The War is won, the work is done, so here's three hearty cheers,
For the outfit that I soldiered with, "The Good Old PIONEERS."

(By One of Them)

From "Philadelphia in the World War, 1914-1919", Philadelphia War History Committee, Wynkoop, Hollenback and Crawford, New York, 1922, Page 773.

ABOUT THE AUTHOR

Margaret M. McMahon has a Ph.D. in Computer Science and Engineering, and with it decades of teaching, public speaking and technical research. She has been a flight test engineer, a consultant, and a college and graduate school professor.

When her son was born, family lines became more relevant and interesting, so she focused her educational skills and talents on her newfound passion to combine family stories with factual records. She is an activist for bringing technology and genealogy together.

She is a frequent speaker in the Washington DC, Maryland and Virginia area. She is the author of "A Week of Genealogy" and "A Weekend of Genealogy".

Email:	aweekofgenealogy@gmail.com
Website:	http://aweekofgenealogy.com
Facebook:	https://www.facebook.com/AWeekofGenealogy
Blog:	http://aweekofgenealogy.com/blog

Made in the USA
Middletown, DE
11 February 2017